sourcebooks

Title:	Brooklyn in Love
Author:	Amy Thomas
Agent:	Jessica Papin Dystel, Goderich & Bourret, LLC.
Publication Date:	February 2018
Category:	Memoir
Format:	Trade Paper Original
Trim:	5.5 x 8.25
ISBN:	978-1-49264591-7
Price:	$15.99 U.S.
Pages:	288 pages

Also available in ebook

Please send all reviews or mentions of this book to the Sourcebooks marketing and publicity departments:

Marketing@sourcebooks.com
Publicity@sourcebooks.com

For sales inquiries, please contact sales@sourcebooks.com
For Librarian and Educator resources visit:
www.sourcebooks.com/library

Sourcebooks

Title:	Brooklyn in Love
Author:	Amy Thomas
Agent:	Jessica Papin
	Dystel, Goderich & Bourret, LLC.
Publication Date:	February 2018
Category:	Memoir
Format:	Trade Paper Original
Trim:	5.5 x 8.25
ISBN:	978-1-4926-4591-7
Price:	$15.99 U.S.
Pages:	288 pages

Also available in ebook

Please send all reviews or mentions of this book to the Sourcebooks marketing and publicity department:

Marketing@sourcebooks.com
Publicity@sourcebooks.com

For sales inquiries, please contact: sales@sourcebooks.com
For Librarian and Educator resources visit
www.sourcebooks.com/library

BROOKLYN IN LOVE

A DELICIOUS MEMOIR OF FOOD, FAMILY, AND FINDING YOURSELF

AMY THOMAS

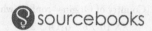

Published by Sourcebooks, Inc.
P.O. Box 4410, Naperville, Illinois 60567-4410
(630) 961-3900
Fax: (630) 961-2168
www.sourcebooks.com

[Library of Congress Cataloging-in-Publication data]

Printed and bound in [Country of Origin—confirm when printer is selected].
XX 10 9 8 7 6 5 4 3 2 1

For Andrew and the peanut.

For making every step, every bite, and
every breath more complete.

And to all the chefs, bakers, barmen and women, and
restaurateurs who unknowingly made our story so
rich and shared your own words and time with me.

"And in almost every dish, you can find, besides the culinary ingredients, the ingredients of a story: a beginning, a middle, and an end."

—Michael Pollan, *Cooked*

"All dreams are crazy. Until they come true."

—Nike ad

Author's Note

Memory is a tricky thing. This is our story as best as I remember, corroborated by Andrew. But it's been written, alternately, under the influence of sugar or alcohol, in a food coma or with postnatal hormones surging through my body, and some details may be blurred as a result.

Introduction

In the fall of 2008, fate walked through my office door.

At the time, I was an associate creative director at the New York office of an international ad agency. A thirtysomething career woman with an active social and dating life, I also moonlighted as a food and travel writer. I dined out more often than I ate in and was obsessed with chocolate, pastries, and all things sweet. Life was good. And then in a Hollywood-scripted moment, the in-house recruiter of my agency asked me what I thought of Paris. Our office there was looking for an English-speaking writer to work on one of France's most iconic luxury marques: Louis Vuitton. Single and thirty-six afflicted with Francophilia and wanderlust, it took but a moment to decide *bien sûr*!

So began two dreamy years in the City of Light (and Dark Chocolate). I built an award-winning portfolio of work and, even better, I got to eat warm *pain aux raisins* for breakfast every day. My commute was hopping on one the city's bikes, the Vélib's, and riding through the Place de la Concorde and up the Champs-Élysées to a stunning Haussmann building with Eiffel Tower views. On the weekends, I tried cooking classes, toured historic boulangeries, and walked miles and miles until the city was mine. With France's generous holiday and vacation policies, I traveled to Portugal, Belgium, England, Italy, and the charming villages and ancient cities throughout France. And the biggest triumph of all was realizing my own personal dream: getting a book contract, which would share some of those very adventures I was having in Paris.

But after three successive contract renewals with my agency, I opted out. I decided I was too old to settle permanently in a foreign city. As wonderful as Paris was, I missed my friends and family back in the States. My carefree life of bicycling and pastry binging in Paris probably wouldn't get any better; maybe I should quit before the Parisians' maddening ability to make things difficult started bringing me down. I deliberated, vacillated and, in a move as bittersweet as when I packed up *for* Paris, I rewound five time zones, swapping macarons and croissants for cookies and doughnuts, and returned to my job and life in New York.

It wasn't an easy transition. In fact, I found repatriating harder than moving abroad. It took me longer to settle back into my comfort zone than it did to adjust to moving to Paris in the first place. I could never shake the sense of being stuck between two cities and loves. Besides, how do you top a life filled with French fashion advertising, daily pastry sampling, and dinners and parties among the chicest human specimens on Earth? After the golden glow of Paris's limestone boulevards, the romantic promise of it all, New York appeared gray, dingy, and harsh.

With a once-in-a-lifetime opportunity behind me and major life goal accomplished, I realized that I had not only closed a chapter of my life, but also seemingly finished the entire first act. Pre-Paris, I had been at the height of my swinging, single thirties. Now, after a couple years romping around Europe, I was staring at the abyss of middle age. Pre-Paris, I had been so focused on getting a book published; now it was written, my mission complete. Pre-Paris, I had been cranking away in advertising without any intentional goals or finish lines. Now, I realized, I'd be hard-pressed to find any accounts at any ad agencies that were better than Louis Vuitton, and my career's finish line seemed uncomfortably close.

On the cusp of forty, I started doing some major soul-searching. If my first act was over, what was act two supposed to look like? A new career? A move to Brooklyn? Another book? Should I cash in all my chips and go on an open-ended, around-the-world adventure? For the first time in eons, I didn't have the answers or a focus. There were no urgent needs or goals. All the go-go-go ambition and adrenaline that had sustained me for two decades risked being relegated to my past. Plodding along in corporate advertising, I felt myself fading to irrelevance and craving something new.

Once the love of my life, New York wasn't getting my heart racing the way it once had—not like food still did. Food was more than a personal obsession and the means to a cushy moonlight gig. It helped chronicle my relationship with the city in which I lived. It was how I organized my itinerary when I traveled. It grounded my social life and became the lens through which I saw and made sense of everything. And it was about to become the landmark for everything that happened in my life.

PART 1

First Comes Love

CHAPTER 1

Alternative American Apple Pie

New York City. Ask people what they love about it, and you'll get any one of a million answers: Broadway shows, world-class restaurants, incredible museums, inspiring architecture. Little Italy, Central Park, SoHo, Wall Street. Top of the Rock, the Empire State Building, the Chrysler Building, the Brooklyn Bridge. Piano bars, sports bars, cocktail bars, dive bars. Diversity, energy, glamour, history. Shopping, boozing, people watching, dancing the night away. Cannoli, cookies, and cupcakes everywhere.

And when you live in the 8.5-million-person metropolis, there are even more nuanced and magical things to love. Dog walkers who deftly carry the leashes of six different sized breeds, all trotting down the street in sync. Window-shopping at Bergdorf Goodman and bargain hunting at Century 21. Kamikaze bicyclists who deliver your pad thai, saag paneer, or spicy tuna rolls at all hours, in any kind of weather. Obsessing about real estate. The way the rising or setting sun cascades down the skyrocketing buildings. Greasy egg sandwiches from the corner bodegas—so dirty but so delicious. The *New York Times*' Sunday Styles section, the *New York Post*'s over-the-top headlines, and Pat Kiernan on NY1. Dining as a competitive sport. The scientists, chefs, poets, entrepreneurs, and socialites on the Ninety-Second Street YMCA's program.

Yet when I returned to New York in the winter of 2011, after two years of working, eating, and embracing joie de vivre in Paris, I wasn't feeling the love. Trying to reacclimatize in the bitterly cold, undeniably filthy city, I couldn't shake my ennui. I couldn't shed the weight I had put on in my final feeding frenzy in Paris, convinced as I had been that I would never have the opportunity to eat freshly baked *pain au chocolat* or hot and melty Nutella street crepes again. And I couldn't evade New York's germs. As soon as I recovered from one illness, I'd get sick all over again, attracting ailments and allergies I'd been immune to my whole life. It wasn't the triumphant homecoming I had envisioned.

More than just feeling physically out of sorts, I felt emotionally adrift. Coming home after two intensely profound and fulfilling years in the most beautiful city in the world was harder than moving abroad to a city where I knew no one. There was no distraction of a foreign culture, no challenge of learning a new language or meeting new people, and no promise of what might be. There was no French romance. I was back in familiar territory, among people, places, and things I knew and had always loved…and yet everything had changed—most of all me.

I had seen, smelled, and tasted new worlds in France. As full as I was with these fresh memories and the wonderful relationships I had developed along the way, they left me with a new emptiness. I was here, they were over there, and all those magical, transformative experiences would never be again. *Poof,* history—an era of my life, gone, and I had been the one to bring it to an end.

It was also difficult because everything in New York had changed in the two years I had been gone. At the agency I returned to, colleagues had been laid off during the financial crisis and the company restructured. Friends had left the city for suburban pastures. And seemingly everyone on the island of Manhattan had gotten married and had a baby. Each change and event was relatively small but added up to a seismic shift in the world I once knew. Everything I remembered that once made me happy now made me uncomfortable. I had pined for New York while in Paris, but now that I was back, I was out of sorts. I was divided, emotionally amiss. My heart belonged to two cities, and now neither of them was entirely home.

Feeling chubby, frumpy, and constantly sick, it wasn't exactly a sizzling dating phase. Nights out with my best friend of thirty years, AJ—who was my partner in crime the years before leaving for Paris but had since gotten hitched and had a baby—were now few and far between. AJ and I did get out for the occasional cocktail, which sometimes led to a late-night flirtation or make-out session in the back of some Meatpacking District club, but mostly my dating life limped along. There was the lawyer—a very decent, kind man, to be sure, but who had such a schlumpy, downtrodden air about him that I was depressed three sips into our first date. The Jersey Boy straight out of central casting with rippling muscles, tats, waxed brows, and perfect veneers, which should have made me swoon but instead just made me giggle. And the supercool Yale alum who was just my speed of preppy and intellectual, and with whom I had several interesting dates—a retro movie at Film Forum, a slow stroll through the Museum of the City of New York, tea in the afternoon. But when the fourth date ended with another deliberately chaste kiss, I realized my passion for him would be best directed elsewhere.

And passion I had in reserves. Dear God, I was bursting with it. I had been secretly keeping track in my head and could no longer deny the sad fact: I hadn't had sex in over a year. Every time I watched *Sex and the City* reruns—as I was wont to do while devouring a pint of Ben & Jerry's on all those cold winter nights, nursing my various colds, ailments, and steadily shrinking ego—I was in awe of the glut of fun, eligible men parading through Carrie's, Miranda's, Charlotte's, and, of course, Samantha's lives. Such variety. Such intrigue and promise. Such testosterone! What had happened in the past ten years? Where did a sister need to go to get laid in New York in 2011?

One night over dinner at Porsena, a small Italian restaurant in the East Village, I recounted my dating misadventures to my friend Joe. The consummate New York bachelor, he was fortysomething, well-to-do, and had impossibly high standards. Joe liked smart, cultured, accomplished women—they just also had to have the face of a Bulgarian fashion model and the body of a yoga instructor, the last point being most essential to him. When he suggested that my teeny chest might be why I didn't have a man in my life, I sat, stunned, two plates of pasta on the table between us, one of which I suddenly envisioned over his head. It was the dumbest, most infuriating thing I had ever heard. It was also the kick in the pants that got me back to online dating.

Once upon a time, online dating was a stigmatized concept, reserved for desperadoes and unsavories. But by now, at least in New York, it was just another place—like the office, a bar, or Whole Foods—to meet people.

Before Paris, I dipped my toe in the pool on Nerve.com, which was a relatively small dating site that attracted edgy, artistic types. At the time, it felt bold and adventurous to be browsing men's profiles as if I were shopping for groceries. But in the years since then, the industry had exploded and the offerings had expanded. Four out of five single people had at least tried it, and one out of six married couples in the United States met online.

Match.com was the biggest site, having started in 1995—when I was wearing double chambray and listening to the Grateful Dead—and now counted millions of members around the world. Other smaller, niche sites joined throughout the years: sites for Jews, Christians, and Ivy Leaguers. Sites for college students and sites for senior citizens. Sites that matched you based on a suggested date, like kayaking in the Hudson River, or your physical location, which led to instant hookups. Sites based on DNA, some for single parents, and others that targeted married people looking for affairs. As one of the founders of OkCupid, a site predicated on answering a series of yes-or-no questions that joined the onslaught in 2009, said in a *New Yorker* article, "We are the most important search engine on the Web, not Google."

My friends actually raved about this OkCupid site, saying it was fun answering all those questions. There were tens of thousands of them, ranging from offbeat and quirky to deadly serious. *Pourquoi pas?* I thought one night at home, glancing down at my A cups that Joe had belittled. Why not enter the fray again? I gathered some photos, entered my stats, and started answering away: Could you date someone who was really messy? Is smoking disgusting? Do spelling mistakes annoy you? And with several dozen surprisingly telling yeses and noes, I was back in the online dating world.

I don't know if it was the increased acceptance of online dating in general or the popularity of this particular site, but the pickings were slimmer. On Nerve, I had met journalists, bankers, producers, designers, scientists—even a Frenchie. I remembered them as articulate, ambitious, and interesting. Where were these natty, witty gents now? The smart but goofy guys? The professional, intriguing, down-to-earth characters? And while I was in cranky old lady mode, what had happened to modesty? Every time I logged in, I struggled to find someone I might enjoy meeting face-to-face. There was so much chest-beating and obnoxious posturing, photos seemingly selected to say, *Here I am on a yacht! Look at all these beautiful people I'm surrounded by! Isn't my life fabulous? Don't you want a piece of this?*

And yet I also didn't want the sensitive, almost effeminate guys I used to go for. Those multi-hyphenate writer slash photographer slash industrial designer slash musicians used to be my catnip. Now I was too old and cynical to hang out in dive bars, encouraging man-boys' dreams of making it big while splitting the bill like a good progressive woman. I had reached a place in my life where I wanted someone who no longer slept on a futon, who owned some decent neckties and shoes, and who didn't balk at spending twenty bucks on a stranger.

The months ticked by. I was winked at—the lazy way of expressing interest online—by guys in their twenties who probably thought they were being sweet by coming on to an older woman. I also received inquiries from earnest men in their fifties and sixties suggesting an afternoon glass of wine. But when it came to the guys in my box—in their late thirties or forties, who appeared well groomed, sounded well informed, and who wrote well in their profiles—well, they were conspicuously absent. The site claimed tens of thousands of users online at any given moment, but for me, it was a desert. But why was I surprised? After all, Joe himself had divulged that he not only trolled for women who were ten to fifteen years younger than him, but he had also shaved eight years off his own age in order to seem a more appropriate match for these ladies. Apparently, if I expected to find love online, I needed to pump up my chest and dial down my age.

It wasn't all dire. One day I had an intriguing message in my OkCupid mailbox. It was a concise note bordering on formal, but it contained just enough intelligence, humor, and modesty for me to click through to the profile. This guy grew up in the Midwest and now lived in Brooklyn. He'd spent time living in France as well as Senegal. He had dark, curly hair and thick-framed glasses. One of his profile photos was an awkward selfie he had taken in his full-length mirror, wearing a black Izod with the collar popped. This was somehow endearing. My fingers tap-tap-tapped my desk as I reread his note. It was another Friday night, *chez-moi*. I was minutes away from a pint of Phish Food and season three of *Sex and the City*—the one when Carrie meets Aidan. I could hear the shrieks of drunk NYU girls outside my East Village apartment and sense my black tabby cat, Milo, waiting for me on the couch. "That's it," I said aloud in my living room, staring at this stranger's photo. "I'm having sex with him."

One week and a couple polite back-and-forth emails later, I was walking down Fifteenth Street to meet my potential seducer. "Andrew?" I asked a bespectacled guy with his nose down in his iPhone outside Park Bar.

"Hi," he said, smoothly sliding the phone in his coat pocket.

"I'm Amy."

"Andrew. Hi...I'm...Andrew," he responded, realizing that had already been established.

"Hi." I smiled, absorbing the awkward moment.

"Shall we?" he asked, gesturing to the door.

Inside, two stools stood auspiciously empty at the bar amid the bustling postwork crowd. I ordered my go-to glass of pinot noir, and after a moment of what looked like indecision or internal debate, Andrew ordered the same.

"So, you were coming from work, I suppose?" he asked, kicking off what was now a routine conversation. Despite my sad track record—or maybe because of it—I had first dates pretty much down: you compared notes about where you lived in the city, what you did for a living, and how you liked spending your free time—about an hour's worth of chitchat. It was rarely romantic or steamy, more like a job interview when you're trying to make a good impression while striking the right balance of talking and listening, coming off as interested but certainly not overeager.

Some guys got off on talking about online dating itself, sharing anecdotes about previous dates gone awry or—it never failed—how crazy New York women are. Others consciously avoided the topic, probably preferring to pretend we had met in a more palatable way. Travel, family, and hobbies indicated broaching intimacy and could lead to revelatory discussions. But everyone had their own tests. I always brought up food and restaurants to gauge a man's awareness of and appetite for what I considered essential topics like Andrew Carmellini's newest venture or which of the swanky Midtown hotel bars made the best manhattan in the city. Andrew didn't rattle off the names of chefs or trendy restaurants when I started waxing poetic about the season's newest crop of hip restaurant openings, but he did share that the best meal he'd had in

New York was at Babbo, Mario Batali's acclaimed three-star Italian restaurant, an instant classic when it opened in 1998, which I saw as very promising.

Our two rounds—a sign that the date was engaging enough not to send one of us packing with a made-up obligation after one drink—were spent talking about writing (he was a legal affairs journalist at an international news agency located in Midtown and a fan of Michael Lewis), living abroad (a Fulbright scholarship had been responsible for his stint in Senegal), and what we did on weekends (he was a big fan of college basketball—not terribly exciting or sexy, but there were worse things). It was just another first date in another bar on another weeknight in the great big bustling city of New York. It had been a nice couple of hours, friendly but benign. So when he leaned in and quickly but firmly kissed me before descending into the Union Square subway station, I was a little surprised. Was he feeling something I wasn't?

Apparently—and fortunately—he was, because our second date was a whole different story.

"So what do you think about Bloomberg?" I asked, intentionally steering the conversation into politics—a potential minefield and telltale topic for detecting irreconcilable differences—halfway into our first drink.

We were huddled against a fogged-up window at an Upper West Side wine bar. Outside, a freak October snowstorm was dumping flakes fast and furiously. I had thought myself so clever when Andrew asked for a second date and I suggested an early evening drink that I'd cram in before a friend's dinner party Uptown. Unsure of this guy, I had wanted to have an easy out. But as the minutes ticked by, I was more and more annoyed that I had to be somewhere in an hour's time. I was feeling cozy and smitten, and wanted to keep gazing at this charming man sitting across from me. He had an awesome head of curly hair, which was becoming increasingly disheveled since he occasionally raked his hand through it. Behind his glasses—which were brainy and preppy, just like his pinstripe button-down—were chocolate-brown eyes.

"You know, he can be a real dick, but I think he's a pretty great mayor in terms of getting things done," Andrew said. It gave me a small thrill when he said "dick," not because I was that horny, but because he otherwise seemed like such a wholesome Midwesterner. I was happy to know he had some edge—or at least the wherewithal to cuss. As he went on about our controversial three-term mayor, the depth of his knowledge impressed me. I kept trying to suppress a smile, feeling like the Cheshire Cat. But if I wasn't mistaken, he was looking pretty content too.

We comfortably drifted into sundried topics like the virtue versus burden of subscribing to the *New Yorker* and whether guys who do yoga are cool or annoying. I learned Bob Dylan was his music hero and shared that Chrissie Hynde was mine. We bantered like friends who hadn't seen each other in months and had so much to catch up on. Yet I desperately wanted to make out with him. We ordered another round of Italian reds served in oversized goblets. I was simultaneously keeping track of and ignoring the time, knowing I was due at my friend's. Finally, I was really late and had to go.

Outside, we huddled under my umbrella. The air was both still from the falling snow and charged with the energy of something unusual happening. Giant flakes cartwheeled beneath the streetlights, and taxis slowly steered up the avenue. We reached the corner and were watching a cab makes its way to us in slow motion when Andrew turned and kissed me. And kissed me. And kissed me. I don't know if it was because it had been so long since I had been properly kissed or if we had amazing chemistry, but the only reason I wanted to leave him and go to this dinner party now was to recount this magical encounter to my friends. Which I did for the rest of the night ad nauseam.

It had been such a great date, I figured I would get a text from Andrew the next day. When I didn't, I thought maybe, in true dude fashion, he was waiting for the start of the workweek. But I heard nothing from him on Monday. When Tuesday came and went without any sort of acknowledgment of the unbelievable time we'd had, I was as furious as I was flummoxed. I was pretty sure I hadn't misread any cues: the knowing glances and smiles, the easy rapport, the heavy make-out session. Why was he blowing me off? Was

I so rusty that the connection I felt was all one sided? Was Andrew out doing this with a different woman every night?

Normally I wouldn't wait for the guy to initiate contact. A proud feminist who grew up watching Martha Quinn and Madonna on MTV and Watts and Tess in *Some Kind of Wonderful* and *Working Girl*, I knew I could do anything that men did. I had no problem popping off an email or text when interested. But I had recently been burned—not once, but twice—thinking I was clicking with a guy only to get ghosted when I reached out after a couple of dates. I was okay being vulnerable, but was over feeling like a fool. Plus, as I got older, I was apparently getting a little old fashioned. Was it really so bad to want the guy to pursue me? I consulted with AJ's husband, Mitchell, who was well versed in modern dating manners. He suggested that I give it one more day and then text Andrew. "Really?!" I asked, exasperated. Mitchell assured me this was the smart play. Begrudgingly, I agreed to humor the male species and wait one more day. Not even two hours later, Andrew called: Was I free Saturday for dinner?

Before long (five dates, to be precise), I made good on my vow to have sex with him, and not long after that, Andrew had sort of become my boyfriend—though I had a hard time calling him that. At thirty-nine, I was more than comfortable being single, independent, and calling the shots. As much as I bemoaned those long months of parking it on the couch, watching sentimental television with my cat and bonbons for company, and as excited as I was to have met Andrew and be devirginized again, I enjoyed my time alone. I was my own person, a whole person, with a rich life. Now that there were certain expectations with Andrew, I realized the difference between the idea of a boyfriend and the reality was a lot of time and emotional investment. Was I ready to do this? Was I ready to do it with him?

Andrew was lovely but lacked an edge. Previous beaux had been wildly romantic in their seduction, filling hotel rooms with flowers, taking me to poetry readings and on motorcycle rides. If I was going to do this, I wanted someone with a little swagger, someone who would take control and wow me. But Andrew was maddeningly methodical, suggesting predictable dinner dates near my apartment in the East Village once, maybe twice a week, for weeks on end. He didn't stray from the script; he never took me by surprise or made grand gestures. Could I really commit to someone who didn't understand that there were amazing restaurants to try beyond one neighborhood? That spontaneity is sexy? That a girl who loves sweets would surely be seduced by a box of truffles—champagne truffles flown in from Switzerland, to be exact? Where was this man's connection with and passion for food?

And yet I was intrigued—just when I'd give up hope, he'd send a text that made me blush or we'd have a conversation that made me feel like we were cut from the same cloth. And the sex kept getting better. I decided I needed some outside perspective; it was time to introduce Andrew to my friends.

Two Sundays later, we joined AJ and Mitchell and Ben, another of my oldest friends, and his girlfriend, Merrill, for brunch, a classic New York tradition and nonthreatening occasion for them to covertly assess this new man in my life. AJ and Mitchell knew the blow-by-blow events of our first couple of months together. They understood my misgivings and insecurities, and I trusted them to tell me if I was being an annoying, hypercritical New Yorker. Ben and Merrill, knowing only that this was the guy I had been dating, would offer a more organic read.

We all met at Jack the Horse, a neighborhood tavern in Brooklyn Heights that has the most incredible smoked trout salad: warm chunks of smoky fish mixed with crunchy almonds, soft fingerling potatoes, and sweet grapes over slightly bitter arugula. It's not your typical brunch fare, but this salad is too good *not* to get at any opportunity, no matter what time it is. The six of us sat at a round table, Andrew's hand on my thigh, my cheeks flushed. This was the first meal with friends in which we were an even number in what felt like eons. I was accustomed to being the third or fifth wheel to AJ and Mitchell and Ben and Merrill. As coffee was refilled and our shared smoked trout salad in the middle of the table was reduced to just a few smears of the thick, creamy dressing, I could tell Andrew was getting high marks for his mild manners and sardonic humor. He made Ben laugh and talked to AJ about the Democratic Party, about which she is fiercely passionate. He asked Merrill just as many questions as she did of him—reciprocating interests and listening skills, no lost arts with this guy!—and Mitchell gave me a subtle thumbs-up across the table.

But it wasn't until Andrew agreed at the last minute to pile into a car with the rest of us and drive across the Gowanus Canal to Four & Twenty Blackbirds, a pie-centric bakery, that all of my friends—and I—were really sold.

When people talk about Brooklyn and its peaceful, verdant streets, they are not talking about Gowanus. In fact, with its sewage-stinking, chemical-slicked canal that is one of the most-contaminated waterways in the country, Gowanus is the butt of many jokes. And yet when sisters Emily and Melissa Elsen were looking for a home in which to open their pie shop, they proudly chose the maligned area that lies between the more family-friendly, picturesque neighborhoods of Carroll Gardens and Park Slope. They vibed off the area's diversity and were prescient enough to know its slow, steady growth was going to transform the area and be good for business.

In 2009, Emily and Melissa were just two ordinary Brooklynites, working, hanging out, and going to friends' dinner parties. They lived in a giant house in Crown Heights—a then-dodgy neighborhood, home to frequent shootings—with a giant kitchen, where they found themselves baking. A lot. It was a natural instinct. Raised in a town of about four hundred in South Dakota, their mother and two aunts ran the only local restaurant, a casual, family-style spot, and their grandmother was enlisted to bake. "Grandma was always a pie maker," Emily recalls. "Pies were her thing." As the sisters riffed and experimented in their Brooklyn kitchen, they too were drawn more and more to pies. Emily explains: "Pie is this durable thing that you can share with people. It's kind of homey and rustic and nostalgic   without being some fancy, decorated confectionary."

Their circle of friends included arty and creative types who frequently hosted dinners and events. The sisters always brought their homemade pies, and soon enough, this led to bona fide baking orders. Their first paid gig was a Valentine's dinner hosted at a friend's loft in Bushwick, for which they made the desserts. "I mean, how much more Brooklyn does it get?" Emily laughs, recounting their early days of being in the epicenter of all things cool and edgy. But the truth was, the Elsen sisters were at the forefront of a swelling Brooklyn foodie movement. Demand for their pies continued, and they kept baking and getting the word out there. "We should start a pie company," Emily recalls saying to her sister. "But we didn't really know what that meant."

As the two continued working at other jobs, they developed and tested recipes, put numbers to paper, and imagined what was possible. It was the cocktail-napkin phase of business development: part dreaming, part doing. Finally, an associate of Emily's at the Gowanus Studio Space, an artists' nonprofit where she worked, tipped her off to a vacant spot she had seen on Third Avenue that might be good for a bakery. Emily went to look at it. She fell in love and started shopping around their quickly assembled business plan. Within a couple months, the sisters had secured a lease with the help of a farm loan guaranteed by their father back in South Dakota.

Then things got really nutty. The Elsens opened in the spring of 2010 and started getting high reviews from the likes of the *New York Times*, *New York* magazine, and *Bon Appétit*. Hundreds of customers came in the first days and cleared them out. "We were floored, *floored*," Emily says of their instant success.

We arrived at Four & Twenty punchy from the car ride over, which reminded me of being back in high school, when we'd cram into someone's Volkswagen for a Blizzard run at the local Dairy Queen. But inside, it was very much of-the-moment Brooklyn: the walls were lined with tin tiles, customers— old-timers reading the communal newspapers, pairs of girls donning beanie hats and fashionable shit-kicking boots in earnest conversation, bearded yet sensitive-looking dudes wearing earbuds and carrying canvas bags—were scattered at wood-plank tables. It was farmhouse hipsterville.

In the back, beneath a chalkboard menu, an open kitchen revealed shelves lined with spices, a couple of heavy-duty refrig-erators, cooling racks filled with baked goods—turnovers, muffins, cinnamon rolls—and one central, stainless-steel table with crocks of rolling pins, whisks, and knives and plenty of room to knead dough. And there at the very front, the half dozen pies on that day's menu sat on display, as homey and inviting as someone's kitchen counter.

Four & Twenty is a seasonal bakeshop—it is Brooklyn, after all, where seasonal, local, and sustainable are the altars at which all foodies worship. The sisters aren't opposed to experimenting with off-season or foraged ingredients but prefer following the popular credo that just so happened to also be their grandma's philosophy: "It just feels better," Emily explains. "Local is so much better and tastier." While they constantly develop new recipes—honey rosemary shoofly, chocolate bourbon mint, strawberry kefir lime—there is one fan favorite that the Elsens make year round: the salted caramel apple pie. In a show of romanticism, Andrew and I decided to split a slice.

Apple pie takes many forms: chunky fruit or dainty slices, oozing with juices, laden with spices, crumbly tops, and moist middles. Without even taking a bite, I knew this was going to be special. The thinly sliced apple rings—visible from the side but obscured from above by thick, sugar-dusted latticework—were densely stacked. Along with a commitment to seasonal fruit and local ingredients, the sisters are hell-bent on having an all-butter crust. "A good crust is a mark of someone who's paid a lot of attention and who cares about what they're making," Emily insists. They don't use Crisco or lard, no margarine or hot oil—just pure butter with a titch of apple cider vinegar to add a little tang, tenderness, and the right flake.

Andrew let me take the first bite. The pie had a perfect amount of give. It was soft and juicy, but not soggy (the downfall of promising slices in lesser hands). Neither sweet nor tart, the salted caramel enrobed the fruit and added a note of savoriness. As promised, the crust was killer.

I'm not normally a pie girl. Tradition doesn't inspire me, and I prefer a bit more decadence—say, Nutella and banana bread pudding sodden with cream or a box of dark Swiss chocolate champagne truffles. But as I looked at my Midwestern man, savoring the collision of flavors and textures in my mouth, I was flirting with becoming a convert.

A quintessential Brooklyn playlist of Arcade Fire, Modest Mouse, and MGMT rocked from the speakers; sunlight streamed through the bars of the windows; and there we sat among my friends at the corner of an enormous communal table. Perhaps I was seeing a new side to him. He *could* be spontaneous. I *would* be surprised and challenged. And he just might be worth the emotional investment. Taking another bite of the thin, firm, slightly acidic layers of apple pie, I felt yet something else tugging at me: happiness to be home in New York.

BRUNCHING
— IN —
BROOKLYN.

At some point, brunch became the weekly social event in New York. Not happy hour, not Saturday night dinner, not birthday parties at Korean karaoke joints, but that Sunday meal once so maligned that no one in their right mind would take this meal seriously. But here we are. It's a thing.

It's not uncommon to wait for ninety minutes or for dancing to break out on the bar or tables after the bottomless mimosas take hold. You could get sucked in for hours and think nothing of dropping a hundred bucks. The worst offenders are in Manhattan, but the hedonism happens in all the boroughs. While you'll probably have some sort of a wait at these Brooklyn spots, you will not have to put up with hooligans or shenanigans.

I obviously love Jack the Horse Tavern in Brooklyn Heights. The smoked trout salad is what lures me back again and again; it's indicative of the offbeat menu that also includes baked eggs, buckwheat pancakes, and a shrimp club sandwich.

Everything at the Farm on Adderly is fresh and tasty. This Ditmas Park pioneer keeps it simple and refined: a smoked pollock cake with harissa mayonnaise, french toast with apple compote, and a kale salad with dried cherries and hazelnuts. Yes, please!

Tucked away in the north of ever-popular Dumbo, Vinegar Hill House feels like you've actually trekked to Vermont. In the rustic ambiance, you can indulge in fancy cocktails along with the oversized sourdough pancake, tarragon-accented omelet, or eggs Benedict topped with pickled onion.

Buttermilk Channel is the ultimate indulgence— pecan pie french toast, Provençal bean stew, a house-cured lox platter. Because of the over-the-top menu and portions, this Carroll Gardens bistro hops all day, every Sunday.

CHAPTER 2

The Intricacies of Artichokes

When I had come home after those two years in Paris, I returned with many things: happy memories of careening around the city on Vélib' bikes and picnicking on Comté cheese along Canal Saint-Martin. Once-in-a-lifetime experiences like seeing Lykke Li perform at an intimate house party filled with bearded *bobos*—Paris's form of hipsters—and presenting my creative campaigns for Louis Vuitton directly to Antoine Arnault, then the fabled brand's communications director, with the Eiffel Tower as my backdrop. I came home with profound new friendships, an expanded cooking repertoire, solid verb conjugation skills, some killer clothes, and...a book contract.

Publishing a book was something I had been working toward for more than a decade. Before Paris, before New

York even, when I lived in San Francisco and started expanding my copywriting career into the editorial world, I had an idea for a book. I wrote a proposal, landed a New York agent, and felt certain that was it: I was on my way. I moved to New York, leaving behind my life and, not inconsequentially, my boyfriend of five years, to pursue this promised life of a young, hotshot writer.

Needless to say, my book went nowhere. I didn't have the background or platform that publishers expected if they were going to invest in me. I wasn't a "somebody" and I didn't have "a name," meaning publicists wouldn't have an easy go of getting me press. I didn't even have experience in the wedding industry, which was the genre of this book I had devoted more than a year to. In retrospect, I was simply young and naive, my hunger for success outweighing my experience. I had to start building my writing career from the ground up.

I set aside my book project and, while still rooted in advertising, developed an editorial career on the side. Instead of boning up on the wedding industry, I focused my free time and energy on pitching and writing articles that schooled me in things I never would have learned otherwise: bespoke perfumers and communication coaches, art exhibitions and interior design, laser hair removal and oxygen facials. I started following my passion for food, writing restaurant reviews and about culinary trends—anything that got me closer to the bakeries, chocolatiers, pastry chefs, and sweets that I loved. It was an exciting time to be covering the local dining scene. With each passing year, eating out in New York became more popular, with chefs like Wylie Dufresne, David Chang, and April Bloomfield ascending in cultural relevance to rock-star status, complete with groupies. Restaurants were the new places to see and be seen; the sooner you went after they opened, the better your bragging rights. Everyone had a smartphone, a blog, and a Twitter account on which to chronicle their dining experiences. Everyone believed their opinions mattered.

It was a fun life. I was a single girl with a side gig that excited me. My relationship with food was deepening. Going out to restaurants became cultural cache. Being part of this world gave me purpose and inspired passion. Food had evolved from something that gave me comfort as a kid to leading me places—Sydney, Sicily, and beyond—I could never have dreamed of going.

I loved what I was doing. But it was also a nonstop hustle. As a freelance writer, you have to constantly dream up new ideas and pitch them to editors, turn new connections into bona fide contacts, and accept rejection—heaping piles of it. You need a thick skin to embrace the reality of moving two steps forward and one step back. For just as soon as you build a relationship with an editor, they'll change jobs without leaving a forwarding address and that hard-earned outlet evaporates. Or you pitch a great idea, get no response, follow up twice, still get no response, and then in the meantime, see the idea published by someone else, making it instantly unsellable.

Since I was still working full-time in advertising, when I did have an assignment, I'd often find myself squeezing in phone interviews in stairwells and taxis, editing pieces on my lunch break, and waking up at 5:00 a.m. and staying up until midnight to meet deadlines. But there were enough triumphs to propel me from indie magazines to glossier national titles, from small front-of-the-book pieces to meatier features, all which stoked my ambition and appetite for more, more, more. A decade after moving to New York, I had written dozens of articles, started a column called "Sweet Freak," launched two blogs, coauthored an interior design book, and I was now facing the holy grail: publication of my very own book, *Paris, My Sweet: A Year in the City of Light (and Dark Chocolate)*.

Which is how I found myself with the food editor of the *New York Post* one chilly February morning, breakfasting on tarte tatin, the lush caramelized apple dessert. We were at Buvette, a wine-bar-slash-restaurant-slash-neighborhood-café that chef-owner Jody Williams had dubbed a *gastrothèque*. She opened it right about the time I came home from Paris and it became one of my instant favorites. It was sort of impossible to not fall in love with the place. It was about as tiny as a typical Manhattan apartment and crammed with charming details: wee menus that had little pop-up illustrations, the sundae-style stacking of cake stands and silver serving trays along the marble bar, an old-timey bicycle featuring a basket of wine corks parked out front. It was as if I had packed up a corner of Paris and transplanted it back in the West Village myself.

I was now enjoying the incredibly generous spread between the editor and me: a thick Belgian waffle obscured by a mountain of fresh cream and berries; crepes stuffed with thick, stick-to-the-roof-of-your-mouth Nutella and daintily folded into quarters; and the tarte tatin, traditionally served as dessert after lunch or dinner but the juicy, caramelized hunks of apple baked beneath buttery puff pastry and topped with slightly sour crème fraîche seemed totally appropriate to be on the table before us at 9:00 a.m. If only every day could start this way.

"It sounds like you experienced a real cultural divide, living in Paris," the editor probed about the torn allegiances between Paris and New York that I had professed in my book. It had now been a year since I returned to New York. While I remained confident in my decision to come home and finally felt I was reconnecting with the city, a little stab inflicted my heart when I thought about Paris and the time I spent there, devouring such things as tarte tatin.

As best I could, I explained some the differences I saw between the two cultures: the French devotion to tradition, their respect for food, the apprenticeships the bakers and chefs go through before becoming full-fledged pros, sometimes learning the trade as adolescents from their own parents. On the American side, there's our penchant for gigantic portions, the experimentation and eccentricity of chefs fusing different styles and ingredients, and the hours we binge on cookbooks, magazines, and TV devoted to food, even if it doesn't translate to actual time spent cooking in the kitchen ourselves. Gazing up at Buvette's chalkboard illustration of the wine regions of France and Italy, I felt like I could talk forever about my time in Paris—both the connections and alienation I had felt there, the love I had developed for the city, and the hole it had left in my heart. But mostly I wanted to savor this experience. After so many years and articles, the tables were turned; I was the interviewee instead of the interviewer. It was a moment.

The nerdy thrill continued over the next couple of months as book launch signings, readings, and celebrations took me to such random places as a library convention in Philly, a Francophile boutique on the Jersey Shore, one of my favorite bookstores in San Francisco, and sweet spots across New York, where friends, family, pastry chefs, chocolatiers, and new fans of my book and blog came out to support me. It was a rush, making me excited for the pinnacle of my book launch activities: a return to Paris, where Mel, my dearest friend in the City of Light, was feting *Paris, My Sweet* at Le Citizen, an eco-chic hotel in the tenth arrondissement. It would be a return to my stomping grounds, the trigger for the entire book—my meaningful journey coming full circle.

So my book was doing pretty well. My relationship, not so much.

Even though my friends liked Andrew and even though I had consciously decided that I'd get serious about finding a relationship once my manuscript was written and submitted, I kept questioning whether he was right for me. I found fault with everything, from his stiff and formal nature and lack of awareness of the city's goings-on to his steady availability and simultaneous lack of planning.

Andrew was laid-back to a fault. He didn't realize that you have to make—sometimes fight for—dinner reservations weeks in advance. He didn't know what movies, museum exhibitions, or concerts were on the horizon. And he didn't seem to care about any of it. This was totally foreign behavior to me, a slave to the city's weekly magazines and up-to-the-minute blogs that dissected every new dish and ounce of current and upcoming culture. And since Andrew didn't seem to have strong opinions about where we ate or what we did, the onus of planning fell to me. Because I did care—very much. In my mind, there was no point wasting a night and a

meal out at a mediocre restaurant. I found myself questioning Andrew's passion and hungering for more connection.
I understood that quibbling about someone's restaurant IQ
seemed shallow, but I had such a strong connection to food
that it was hard to overlook.

The publication of my book only seemed to exacerbate
my uncertainty. After having been single for the better part of
the past decade, in two cities, through three jobs, over dozens
of trips, weddings, birthdays, and illnesses, it was hard to
share my weekends, my plans, and, now, my dreams with
someone else. Andrew was very complimentary and excited
for me when my book came out. But he hadn't been there for
its long journey to publication. He didn't have the history,
didn't know the players, and hadn't been there for my ups
and downs, fears, and triumphs. I knew I should have been
grateful for his support and presence, but instead I wanted to
embrace this moment on my own. This book was something
I had worked so hard toward for years. This guy had been
around for four months. Was it really that ridiculous to feel
reluctant to share this achievement with someone who may
or may not work out?

My seesawing emotions inevitably affected the relationship, which all came to a head one night after what should
have been a divine dinner.

We had gone to Il Buco Alimentari e Vineria, a new restaurant inspired by the rustic sensibility and languid lifestyle

of Umbria. The papers and blogs had been gushing about the NoHo (North of Houston Street) newbie's house-cured charcuterie, fresh baked breads, and homemade pasta, and Andrew and I finally had a reservation (which I had made—*not that I was keeping track*). The restaurant was a spin-off of Il Buco, a dark and moody, antiques-filled Italian spot that had been a romantic date destination since 1994. Il Buco's owner, Donna Lennard, was a real neighborhood pioneer, owning both a home and business in the area, which wasn't considered desirable for either. She and her partners had been casually looking for another space in the neighborhood for a few years where they could create an Italian emporium. They wanted to sell products from Italy and, more important, "I wanted a place to bake bread," Donna says, a woman after my own heart. "That was the biggest impetus." Even so, she was in no hurry to open something new. "If it happens, it happens," she figured, unwilling to let a new endeavor in the topsy-turvy restaurant world interfere with the ease or well-being of her and her family's lives.

And yet, in 2010, it happened. The partners found a space that had everything they were looking for just one block away from Il Buco. NoHo was by then well on its way to being a popular enclave of designer condos, upscale boutiques, and other trendy restaurants—a million proverbial miles from the dark and seedy streets that were once home to vagabond artists and strung-out addicts. "Change is double edged,"

Donna philosophizes, reflecting on the neighborhood's old, grittier charms while embracing the integrity it has retained, like the landmarked buildings and iconic cobblestone streets. Alimentari e Vineria itself, with its two floors of dining and gourmet market peddling cheese, gelato, and pantry items like Pugliese tomatoes, salted sardines, and olive oils, is all hidden behind a modestly canopied facade. Blending an old-world feel and modern bustle, it was instantly at home in the neighborhood.

Now, tucked at a small table on the second floor, I was forcing myself to enjoy the evening I had been so looking forward to. Conversation between Andrew and me felt forced. There wasn't a flow or nice, easy rhythm. It wasn't fun or titillating. All the other diners seemed to be laughing merrily or having deep, thoughtful tête-à-têtes. We were stilted, as if we were bluffing. Both of us knew something was off between us, yet neither of us had the courage to confront it. Andrew sat so ramrod straight in his chair that I was suppressing an annoyance that discomfited me with its fierceness when I should have been letting the heavenly, crispy artichokes—one of the dishes all the reviews had been raving about—take me away.

Artichokes aren't something I especially love. You don't even see them on many menus, probably because you have to really *want* them to make them work. They have sharp outer leafs that protect their tender hearts, the prized bit of the unique vegetables that are worth really savoring. After Donna described the way her kitchen prepares them, I understood how time- and labor-intensive the classic Roman dish is.

First, the hearts have to be freed from those tough outer leaves with a sharp paring knife. They're then soaked, so they lose their inherent bitterness, and are marinated for flavor. Finally, the hearts are gently fried until they're both crisp and tender, before being finished off with a grating of dehydrated lemon peel. They arrive, just a small antipasto, and may not seem like a lot but, man, some serious devotion went into making them.

Did I have that kind of patience and tenderness in me?

Despite our agonizing charade over dinner—after the artichokes came fat spears of fried polenta, slices of unctuous octopus, and forkfuls of *cacio e pepe* along with more stilted conversation and suppressed frustration—I invited Andrew back to my place. Once away from the bustling cheer of the restaurant and the city's electric energy, I couldn't ignore the awkwardness anymore. "Is everything okay?" I asked as Andrew took a tentative seat on the edge of my green velvet loveseat.

"I was going to ask you the same thing. You seem a little tense or something."

"*I* seem tense?" I retorted. "You've been so stiff all night."

My heart started picking up speed. As much as I hate pretending things are fine when they clearly aren't, I will do just about anything to avoid confrontation. Andrew, at least tonight, seemed more comfortable with it.

He let out a small sarcastic laugh. "Okay. I probably *was* stiff all night. Because something is going on with you. Not just tonight. I've been getting all kinds of mixed messages lately."

"What are you talking about?"

"Like at your launch party—which, let's be clear, you invited me to—you barely said a word to me. And afterward, when we went out for a drink with your friends, I just felt like you didn't even want me there."

"Well," I sputtered, "I'm sorry that I have to talk to everyone else at these events. You know they've supported me and are part of the book, and it makes me happy to have them there."

"Right. I guess that's the thing," Andrew said. "Sometimes it doesn't seem you're happy to have *me* there."

"Don't be ridiculous." I rolled my eyes and crossed my arms across my chest.

"I'm not, Amy." Andrew was totally calm, looking at me straight on. "Are you? Are you happy to be with me? Because if you're not, there's no purpose for any of this."

His question threw me for a loop. I *was* happy to be with Andrew—just not all the time. It felt suffocating to have to think about another person's needs and emotions. Would he fit in at the events with my friends? Would he be comfortable and have people to talk to? Was I paying him enough attention? I didn't want to be responsible for him. I just wanted to enjoy this accomplishment without anything, or anyone, getting in the way. But how could I say any of this?

"Well, I guess your silence is my answer." Andrew snapped me back to the moment.

"No, I was just... I was thinking." Quickly, I tried sorting through the colliding thoughts inside my head. "I am happy," I hedged, putting a tentative hand on his leg, trying to offer some reassurance—for him or myself, I'm not sure. "It's just... It's hard," I finished lamely.

"Hard? What's so hard?"

I opened my mouth again to explain that this relationship was so new and, while he was a great guy, I didn't know if this was it, so I was trying to keep some sort of distance or barrier in case things didn't work out...and then I could bail. That I liked him but really liked my independence too. That, bottom line, I had doubts, serious doubts. Since I couldn't find a diplomatic way to articulate that, instead I offered, "I dunno."

"Well, I guess I shouldn't have bought that ticket then," Andrew sputtered, both flushed and flustered. He remained on the edge of the couch, looking down at his hands clasped between his legs like a schoolboy who had been caught doing something naughty.

My heart, which had been thawing from its cold state just a moment ago, abruptly stopped. My ears were getting all red and fiery. *Oh no. He didn't.* I was chanting to myself. *No, he did NOT!* I asked, "What are you talking about?"

"You invited me to go to Paris with you next month," Andrew said. "So I bought a ticket."

Dumb silence. I didn't know what to say. I had told him about Mel's party and we had talked about going to Paris together. But that was it: a tepid invitation. And that had been weeks ago. Neither of us had come within an inch of mentioning it again. And now he had gone and bought an airplane ticket without a word? How passive-aggressive could you get?

"Seriously?" was all I could muster. Which I guess was more than enough.

Andrew finally burst, contending that I had invited him, so WTF? Why was I always acting like I didn't want him around? Why was I so hot and cold? Why was I even dating him to begin with?

As he went on, unleashing weeks of frustration, I felt both bad and relieved. After all, I did like him. I really, really did. Andrew was the first guy in years who I thought there was potential with. Something in the back of my head kept telling me to give this time, to give him a chance. There was something here worth giving in to, despite my reservations and resistance.

I knew I was being a jerk not hanging out with him more

at the launch events or when I withheld information about going out with friends. I knew I was being a jerk in a lot of ways. And though I didn't say as much out loud, I did apologize to him. As maddeningly steady, available, and oblivious as he could be, I knew Andrew's heart was gold—a rare and beautiful thing, a near miracle in New York City. Him putting me on the spot and voicing his own frustrations had diffused my ire. The agitation that had been festering inside me now leaked out like from a sad, noxious party balloon.

When Andrew got up to leave, I barely had the strength or heart to walk him to the door. I somehow managed to broker a tentative truce, asking him to please be patient with me, but he was nonplussed. I had to figure out what I was doing, what I wanted. He may have had a heart of gold, but as I was learning, there was more going on behind his laidback demeanor than met the eye. He was no pushover, and he deserved some clarity.

He left without so much as a kiss, the heavy door clicking behind him. I stood listening to him walk down the carpeted hallway of my apartment building. I heard the elevator *ding* and then its doors swooshed shut, taking Andrew back out into the New York night and leaving me alone—presumably as I wanted to be.

Well, I thought, as I locked the door and dragged my sorry ass toward the bedroom, suddenly exhausted, *I guess he's coming to Paris.*

ROMANTIC
— ITALIAN —
RESTAURANTS

Italian restaurants are the stuff romantic dates are made of. Usually. If you think about it, it's a formula that works: a cozy room full of dark, earthy woods; menus that indulge with multiple courses of carbohydrates; plus servers with seductive accents who deliver the food with knowing looks. As they say, that's amore.

All of these restaurants define themselves as Tuscan or Northern Italian, which means you can count on them for amazing house-made pastas along with classic meat and fish dishes.

The original Il Buco is actually much more romantic than Alimentari e Vineria, owing to its mismatched antiques, walls lined with wine bins, and copper cookware hanging overhead.

Il Cantinori has graced the Village since 1983. Wood-beamed ceilings, white linen tablecloths, and a front that opens onto the sidewalk create a classic Tuscan ambiance.

People start lining up outside Park Slope's al di la Trattoria before the restaurant even opens for dinner service. It's a narrow corner spot, dominated by a bold maroon-and-yellow color palette, with exposed brick walls that give the room a warm glow.

Another cramped corner location that is a neighborhood favorite is Rucola in Boerum Hill. Tables are wedged tightly together, so prepare to feel quite cozy. Cocktails are surprisingly unique, and a farm-to-table credo rules.

Located within a century-old pharmacy that is still decorated as such, Locanda Vini e Olii in Clinton Hill is lively and fun while still managing to be a sweet spot for two.

CHAPTER 3

Revelatory Chicken

There's something magical about returning to a city you love. It's a special rush to be back in the streets that hold such distinct memories, visiting favorite restaurants, bakeries, and chocolatiers. Your body remembers, and your psyche comes alive. It's like coming home and hugging your mom after not seeing her for months and months—a primal form of comfort and joy.

This is how it was being back in Paris that week in April. Andrew and I were both on our best behavior, trying to nudge the relationship along and make the most of the international jaunt, despite its inauspicious beginnings. Inevitably there were moments as we walked along the narrow streets that I longed to explore the city on my own, the way I used to, but it was mitigated by the joy of having someone—a "lovah" in the language of Carrie Bradshaw—to share the romance of the City of Light.

Andrew and I sipped champagne cocktails at the cozy Hemingway Bar, tucked in the back of the Ritz, just before the grand hotel closed for renovations for three and a half years. He introduced me to wine from France's eastern Jura region when we indulged in a three-course lunch at Bistrot Paul Bert, a beloved neighborhood restaurant in the eleventh arrondissement. At Chez L'Ami Jean, a raucous Basque restaurant in the seventh, we gushed over the most heavenly lobster bisque, poured tableside with requisite French fanfare, and were charmed by two octogenarian couples sitting at a table close enough to us that we might as well have sat together. Each meal was so languorous and indulgent, so different emotionally and literally from the wham-bam intensity back home.

Andrew was proving himself to be the perfect travel companion. He smiled through the lovely book party that Mel threw on a beautiful night beside the canal, content to make small talk with not one person he knew. He was delighted to accept the invitation to have Sunday dinner with one of my old colleagues and his family at their country home. But the best part of Andrew being there in Paris was having someone to share pastries with. From Boulangerie Julien to Du Pain et Des Idées to every local boulangerie in between, with their rows of flawless éclairs and tartlettes and baskets of golden croissants beckoning from the windows, we sampled and *mon dieu*'d. I got to taste everything that I love and had been missing—but in small enough portions to ensure that my jeans would still zip when it was time to return to New York. And before I knew it, the week that had caused so much tension was coming to a close. Andrew's plane departed a day before mine, and when his taxi pulled away from the curb, I hopped on a Vélib' to enjoy my last day and night in Paris solo. From one lovah's arms to another's.

We had been back in New York for a good week with neither of us urgently trying to see the other. While the trip had been a success overall, it was fair to say Andrew and I both needed a little space after being together twenty-four-seven and the drama leading up to it. For all I knew, he was over me and my noncommittal bullshit.

What are you doing thurs night? Andrew texted.

Oh good, it appeared he wasn't over me. No plans.

Dinner? Barbuto? 8? Well, well, well. I liked this confident tone. And I liked his choice. Barbuto is New York dining at its best. It's a respected restaurant that bustles with cool people who are there to enjoy the laid-back vibe and Italian cooking done with a fresh, modern California spin.

Sounds great. I fired back. C u there!

Two nights later, Andrew and I were sitting beside one of the restaurant's garage-door walls that slide up in the summer, a throwback to the space's former life as a garage. We had selected a bottle of wine (Barbera d'Alba), strategized our order (one antipasto, one primi, and one secondi, split between the two of us), and were settling into a nice mood. Unlike that night at Alimentari e Vineria, we were both relaxed, conversation was easy, and, best of all, I was genuinely happy to be with him. Things felt good. I was grateful that we seemed to have weathered the storm.

"So, I know it's been hard for you." Andrew turned serious sometime between the cavatelli and the chicken, putting his elbows on the table and leaning toward me. He peered at me through his glasses, his eyebrows moving expressively above the frames. "You're maybe a little unsure or feeling pressure to know what you want. And I know there are things I could probably do differently; I know I'm not perfect. But I'm really trying because—well, I know you and I are a good thing. The fundamentals are strong, and if you believe in that, then we're good."

Gulp. I took another sip of wine while Andrew surged on. "I just feel like we really get along—it's easy and fun. We laugh. I can talk to you. I always have a good time with you, which is why I wanted to go to Paris to begin with." Despite myself, I was getting a little misty eyed. After all these months, it was rare that Andrew and I opened up and exposed any emotion. We could talk about all kinds of stuff, which was one of my favorite things about him—we had great conversations. But it was usually, well, more conversational stuff: the state of journalism and publishing; the prospects of the KU Jayhawks, his alma mater's basketball team, and the Red Sox, my beloved baseball losers; the Stones versus the Beatles. And here he was, out of nowhere, being so open and direct. Confident but earnest. I knew he had deliberated about what to say, which made me appreciate it even more. "I'm listening, and I'm learning. I really want this to work out, and I'm willing to do whatever it takes."

I nodded but wasn't sure what to say. I didn't know where this surge of openness was coming from. Without really thinking, I baldly asked, "What do you want?"

Andrew looked squarely at me. "I want to spend more time with you," he said. "I want to *live* with you."

Say what? My carb-loaded stomach lurched, but not in the typical way. If it had been a few weeks ago, such a proclamation would have had me running for the exit. But tonight was different. I felt strangely calm as heat crept up my neck. Did this guy really still like me? *Could* he still like me? Was there some fateful reason we were still together? Instead of feeling trapped or threatened by the emotion Andrew expressed, I realized the lurching in my gut was more akin to butterflies. Contrary to my conflicting feelings of the past couple months, I felt myself blushing. "Really?" I asked.

Andrew leaned in and kissed me. I remembered the shivers I had felt when we'd first kissed during that October snowstorm, and the loopiness I couldn't contain for days afterward from having met the most incredible guy. From the excitement that my patience seemed to have finally paid off in the form of a smart, handsome, thoughtful man. It made me question what had I been doubting all these months. Big deal if he didn't religiously follow restaurant openings or the latest stories of chef meltdowns that lit up the Twittersphere. So what if his biggest passion wasn't ramp season at the farmers' market or chronicling the city's ramen shops. He had compassion and perseverance, and continuously dragged me out of my comfort zone, challenging my idea of what I thought I wanted. And I was discovering, he actually had a really good palate.

Andrew pulled back and we sat staring at each other, a fragile bubble of hope and possibility enveloping us. And just when I thought the moment couldn't get any more beautiful, our waitress descended on the table with a dish of steaming, aromatic chicken. "Here we are!" she sang. "The *pollo al forno*."

Chicken is like vanilla ice cream. It can be dreadfully boring and uninspired, and, let's face it, it often is. But put in the right hands—like those of Chef Jonathan Waxman, California cuisine pioneer, two-time *Top Chef Masters* contestant, James Beard Award winner for Best Chef: New York City, and chef-owner of Barbuto—and it becomes transcendent. In fact, in the four decades of his career, he has made an art out of cooking chicken.

Jonathan's career started in an unlikely way back in the seventies. By his early twenties, he had already been a trombone player, a bartender, and a salesman at a Ferrari dealership. The car dealer's wife was a foodie (though they didn't use that word back then, Jonathan points out), and after their many conversations about cooking and restaurants, she suggested that he explore his passion. "So the head mechanic and I decided to take a food class together," Jonathan remembers wryly.

The class, at Tante Marie in San Francisco, delighted Jonathan. "I loved every minute of it," he says. The instructor, like the dealer's wife, clearly saw his passion and thought Jonathan should be a chef. So much so that, unbeknownst to him, she signed him up at La Varenne, a then-new cooking school in Paris.

Jonathan took the bait and arrived in Paris in 1976, never having been to Europe, not knowing the language or anyone in the city. But he found a roommate, made friends, learned to cook, and toured the three-star restaurants of France. Discovering he indeed had a knack inside the kitchen that his earlier teacher had intuited, he returned to the West Coast after finishing La Varenne and worked stints at Chez Panisse in Berkeley and Michael's in Santa Monica, two seminal restaurants of the era. At both establishments, he played a pivotal role in shaping what we now know as California cuisine, which relies on simple techniques and fresh, local ingredients.

In 1984, Jonathan left California and made his way to New York City, where he opened Jams on the Upper East Side. The restaurant was iconic. A hot spot. It had an open kitchen, a minimalist aesthetic, and bright, fresh food—all new to the New York dining scene, which was still dominated by stuffy fine dining. For years, the restaurant and Jonathan were at the center of an exciting movement. Critics cooed, celebrities feasted, and business boomed. Then the 1987 stock market hit and, soon after, Jams closed. Jonathan moved back to California for a spell, opening a couple other restaurants and doing consulting work before returning to New York and reclaiming his spot in the city's dining scene.

Not long after opening a well-received restaurant, Washington Park on lower Fifth Avenue, Jonathan's Italian neighbor, owner of Industria Superstudios in the West Village, pressed him to check out a vacant space in his building, where he suggested Jonathan should open a new Italian joint. Jonathan wasn't keen. By that point in his career, he had launched six restaurants. He was over the scene. Italian was what he cooked at home, not for the public. And yet he went to see the space, and he finally relented to his neighbor's pressings. "Fuck it," Jonathan remembers saying, "we'll just do it."

Jonathan demolished the space, originally a car garage, salvaging only the doors that roll up to the outside world along its two exterior walls. Keeping things raw, aesthetically and philosophically, he didn't sink a lot of investment into Barbuto. He didn't hire a manager or install a point of sale system, essentially expecting the restaurant to fail. "It was a mom-and-pop sort of place," Jonathan remembers. "And I was the mom *and* the pop."

But Barbuto was instantly successful. "It was packed from the very beginning," Jonathan says, and momentum has only built over the years. Things got a little "hairy" during the 2008–2009 financial crisis, but when Jonathan appeared on Bravo's *Top Chef Masters* right after that, business nearly doubled.

Which brings us back to his chicken.

"Not to sound arrogant, but most people just don't know how to cook chicken." It's different from steak or fish, Jonathan points out, when you're just preparing part of the animal—a fillet. Cooking the whole thing can be daunting.

"Every chicken is different," the chef points out. "You have to look at each one individually." Which is what he does hundreds of times over. "We sell so much chicken, it's absurd," he says dryly, acknowledging the restaurant goes through five or six hundred birds a week in the summertime.

Jonathan had been celebrated at his original Jams restaurant for the deboned, grilled half chicken he served with fries. "But it was a different beast," he says, in comparison to the *pollo al forno* at Barbuto, which is now one of the city's most iconic dishes.

"I wanted to not waste anything," he says of the choice to roast the bird on the bone at Barbuto. Placing two halves of a chicken in a skillet, he dresses them with olive oil, sea salt, and fresh cracked pepper. He then roasts it in the wood-burning oven, basting it along the way to make succulent, brown, and crispy skin. Beneath, the meat becomes tender and juicy. After letting the pieces rest for a few minutes, he tops them with *salsa verde*, a mixture of smashed garlic, capers, cured anchovies, olive oil, salt, pepper, and a mash of herbs—such as parsley, tarragon, and oregano—and serves it so simply and yet it's so spectacular.

"It became one of my greatest hits," Jonathan acknowledges. "And when people love something, you don't deny them."

In the weeks following that revelatory dinner, I found myself in long-forgotten territory. A goofy grin came to my face when I thought of Andrew. A speeding up of my heart. That telltale fluttering in the belly. He was under my skin. I looked forward to seeing him more often—I *wanted* to see him more often. I was no longer protecting my free time or strategizing like some weird misanthrope about how not to include him at group dinners. I wanted him there, with me, all the time. I wanted friends to get to know him, to unearth his sense of humor as I currently was, to be charmed by his gravelly voice and wholesome manners, to meet the man who could drop facts about the Supreme Court, the Civil War, and the history of Pearl Jam with equal aplomb. I caught myself daydreaming like a fourteen-year-old: about how cute he had been on AJ's birthday when he unselfconsciously gave the Lower East Side hipsters a run for their money as we wound up dancing in a subterranean bar, about how we unabashedly made out in the crowded East Village streets, NYU students telling us to get a room. I longed to see him minutes after we parted. Yep, I felt it—I was in love with this guy.

As soon as I let go of my hang-ups, I opened up to Andrew and all the possibilities of being with him. To be fair, it wasn't like I woke up one morning in a rapturous aha moment. It was work. It took time. It was with the help of my brilliant therapist that doubt was replaced by hope, and I started moving toward him instead of trying to keep distance between us. Living together still seemed a bit much, but little by little, as I continued slogging through my personal baggage and unfair expectations, things changed.

Our dynamics became so much more natural and fluid. I was no longer checking off all the things he wasn't, but was psyched about what, and *who*, he was: kind, independent, no bullshit, intuitive, generous, and up for anything. Plus, he had a great bum and was superaffectionate, always putting his hand on the small of my back or lightly rubbing his thumb across my wrist. It was finally how I imagined having a boyfriend would be: a fun, fulfilling enhancement to my life, not rocks in my pockets, threatening to take me downstream.

And then suddenly we were just like all those other New York couples who had unknowingly taunted me for so long. Going out Saturday nights naturally meant waking up the next day to sex and brunch. I became one of those girls at a crowded restaurant on a Sunday morning with a shit-eating grin and a big pile of pancakes, disheveled hair pulled back in a knot, wearing last night's clothes and smudged eyeliner.

As spring blossomed into summer, we started upping the ante. I was working on an article about Connecticut's coastline, so we hopped in a rental car in Midtown and drove north to my home state. Through the tall hedges hiding regal estates in Greenwich, the urban-chic villages of Westport and Darien, to my neck of the woods—the beatnik clam shacks and weathered seaside cottages of southeastern Connecticut—we cruised the coastline. We pulled over to taste-test lobster rolls, went kayaking in the tributaries of the Connecticut River, and watched the sunset on the tiny peninsula town of Stonington. My love for the area was deeper than ever before as I shared it with someone who newly saw its charm and beauty.

We spent the weekend at my dad's, where Andrew bantered wit for wit with the man whom every boyfriend has ever had to measure up to—and he held his own. We went to my cousin's for an impromptu party and he was totally comfortable, nonchalantly chatting with all my cousins, aunts, and uncles who ranged in age from two to seventy, and decibel levels of one to eleven. And it was so easy. Andrew *made* it easy.

The summer continued with a trip to Colorado for his friend's wedding, where we also went hiking, mountain biking, and ghost chasing at the Stanley Hotel, the allegedly haunted hotel that inspired Stephen King's *The Shining*. We took a train up the Hudson River to a cute bed-and-breakfast for an extended weekend of loafing, reading, and tennis. Feeling more adventurous and certain about our future, we booked a trip to Buenos Aires for the following spring. And throughout it all, we explored Brooklyn with equal excitement.

It was partly because Andrew lived in Sunset Park, an as of yet ungentrified neighborhood dominated by Mexican and Chinese immigrants near the exquisitely landscaped

Green-Wood Cemetery, so many weekend mornings would start there. But it was also because I had my sights on defecting from Manhattan to this gentler, greener borough.

I had fallen in love with Brooklyn Heights when I came home from Paris for AJ's wedding two years earlier. One of the oldest and most landmarked neighborhoods—in fact, it was the first entire neighborhood in New York City to be protected by the Landmarks Preservation Commission—it sits immediately across the East River from downtown Manhattan, offering million-dollar views of the skyline, Statue of Liberty, Brooklyn Bridge, and constant, whirling helicopters taking tourists and bankers to and fro. Instead of a fancy rehearsal dinner, AJ and Mitchell had thrown a party in one of the neighborhood's quintessential Federal town houses with exposed brick and ten-foot-tall windows—the kind of place that makes you want to grow roots and stay there the rest of your life. We had spent the afternoon of the party food shopping at the local grocery and liquor stores. Everyone we passed in the street seemed part of a true community, greeting each other, pausing to stop and pet each other's dogs and say hello to their children by name. Even though I was single at the time and living in the most exquisite city of Paris, it captured my heart and became an indelible image of where I saw my life going. I decided I would trade my frenetic East Village digs upon my return for this quieter, more…well, mature part of the city.

As Andrew and I ate our way through every weekend that summer, I was expanding my knowledge beyond Brooklyn Heights. We'd wake up at his place, grab a Mexican coffee—made ridiculously sweet with condensed milk topped with sugar—and hit the pavement.

We window-shopped along Court Street, the closest thing Brooklyn has to Manhattan, perusing the indie clothing boutiques, bookstores, and Italian bakeries, and stopped at Frankies 457 Spuntino, a casual Italian restaurant that every young Brooklynite loves, to pound fresh ricotta, gnocchi, and meatballs. Afterward, I dragged us ten blocks out of the way to hit up Sugar Shop, a modern-retro candy store I loved, to load up on malt balls and gummies.

We strolled the magnificent blocks of Victorian homes and green lawns in Ditmas Park, as if suddenly transported from the city's whirl to a faraway college town, perusing the rhubarb, Bibb lettuces, and buckets of fresh clams at the farmers' market, before demolishing fried egg sandwiches on ciabatta at the Farm on Adderly, one of the borough's now-prolific farm-to-table restaurants.

We shared pizza at Franny's: one red, one white, both pockmarked with giant charred blisters from the exceedingly hot brick oven. In a borough known for its temples of pizza worship, Franny's is right up there, owing to the perfect flavors oozing from each simple ingredient, from the milky mozzarella to the salty-sweet tomato sauce to the briny black olives.

We pit-stopped for midday cocktails at Lavender Lake in Gowanus, the back patio blessedly empty in the heat of summer; we sought out the dark, nearly windowless cavern that is Park Slope's Union Hall, sipping amber pints of IPA and watching bocce players trying to knock each other's balls.

We even made it to the holy mecca of Brooklyn food fanaticism: Smorgasburg, a collection of food vendors that battle it out for the most outrageously delicious, ridiculously inventive food. We duly ate our heads off, sampling panko-crusted chicken sandwiches topped with pickled cucumbers and daikon, brown butter cookies doused in flakes of sea salt, and the coup d'état—gigantic, billowy doughnuts from a Bed-Stuy bakery called Dough, one sweetly flavored with hibiscus, the other a savory, roasted café au lait varietal.

I was thrilled with it all: not only all these delicious, new brunches and cocktails and sweets, but the landscapes we crossed to find them and the conversations Andrew and I had along the way. I loved how the occasional old-relic clapboard house would stick through the otherwise uniform brownstones, transporting me to a different city and era. I was enchanted by the giant plane trees that made the slate sidewalks ripple with their bulbous roots that had been grow-ing for centuries and the gas lanterns along the gently slop-ing, quietly humming streets. I laughed at the dollhouse-size homemade lending libraries filled with paperbacks that stood at some curbs, and the way people left old blenders, records, shoe trees, and other bric-a-brac items on their stoops, free for the taking. From Prospect Heights to Red Hook to even Brooklyn's commercial downtown, I couldn't help but notice a different kind of energy everywhere: the mishmash of languages, races, clothing styles, and ages. There was a rhythm and a beat to it all. Exotic yet old school. Hippie and hip-hop. Dynamic yet relaxed. Walking arm in arm with Andrew, taking it all in, our bodies seemed just the right size and speed for each other and Brooklyn seemed destined to be my future.

As summer drew to a close and Andrew and I were delaying separating at the end of another lovely weekend of traversing Brooklyn, I could tell something was on his mind. Or maybe it was me and this giant elephant in the room. Along our explorations, we'd occasionally stumble upon an open house and pop in, nosing around a stranger's apartment. Andrew knew that I intended to move to Brooklyn, so there was good reason to be checking out these open houses. Things were now going so well between us, and yet I was looking for a one bedroom that fit only my preferences, tastes, and needs. It was, how do you say? *Awkward.* That morning, we had popped into a random Park Slope open house and the voyeuristic thrill that usually accompanied me was conspicuously absent.

"Sooo…" I said, turning to Andrew on a grimy corner of Fourth Avenue near Barclays Center, where I would catch my train back to Manhattan.

"Sooooo," he responded, smiling at me, hands encircling my waist.

"I guess it's getting a little weird looking at open houses together."

Andrew looked up at the sky, nodding his head. "Yeah. A bit," he said. "The question is: What do we do about it?"

"Well, either we stop going to open houses together, or we start planning to live together," I offered, emboldened by how good and how right things felt between us.

So there on the corner, beneath a late-summer sun, we talked about how it would be great to live together…just not yet. Nine months of dating might be more than enough time for some couples to pull the trigger, but we were two individuals who had lived alone for so long that any excitement associated with the prospect of cohabitation was tempered with just a little bit of terror. With a combination of my Germanic discipline and his Midwestern patience, we agreed I would put my apartment search on hold and we'd look together in the New Year. It was a huge step. I had envisioned a home for myself in Brooklyn for a long time. That I could imagine doing it with Andrew told me this was real. The relationship was going places. I had a future with Andrew. In Brooklyn.

FRENCH INVASION

I was a Francophile even before living in Paris for two years. Needless to say, when I came home to New York in 2011, I was thrilled to find a French invasion underway.

About nine months after I returned, Ladurée, the famed tea parlor that is purportedly responsible for creating the macaron, opened on the Upper East Side. Immediately there were lines stretching down Madison Avenue, as hordes of ladies who lunch and Japanese tourists patiently waited for their boites of pretty pastel pastries from the teeny storefront. When a second location, a grand salon, opened in SoHo a few years later, the hysteria had subsided, making it easier to get a fix of lemon meringue tarts, mille-feuille, Mont Blanc gâteaux, or any other storybook creations.

Famed baker Éric Kayser has proven more than anyone that you can find the best tastes of Paris in New York. His first bakery arrived in New York in 2012, and there are now ten Maison Kayser locations between Manhattan and Brooklyn serving up baguettes, brioche, and crumbles that will make you say "Miam!"

Dominique Ansel, another Parisian transplant, became known to the world when he invented the

Cronut in 2013, two years after opening his eponymous bakery in SoHo. The croissant-doughnut hybrids get all the fanfare, but the pastry chef's versions of the Kouign-amann, Paris–Brest, and even New York cheesecake all warrant a trip.

Pastry chef Damien Herrgott, who had once worked for France's "Picasso of Pastry," Pierre Hermé, is at the helm of Bosie Tea Parlor (where I had the honor of having my book launch party). Though lesser known than the actual French imports, Damien churns out stellar viennoiseries—croissants, pain aux chocolat, chausson aux pommes—and gâteaux, like the Ispahan, a raspberry-and-rose-flavored cake that is one of Pierre Hermé's most-celebrated offerings in Paris.

CHAPTER 4

Forty Turns of the Carrot Grinder

With the decision to move in together made but the actual search for an apartment still a few months down the road, Andrew and I reveled in our relationship. We were starry eyed. Publically affectionate. In love. Eating up the city.

It was nauseatingly great. So why was I feeling so adrift and uncertain?

While this was the first time in nearly a decade I had relaxed into a relationship and allowed myself to feel hopeful, confident, and loved, I was otherwise feeling insecure. In fact, I was floundering. The self-assuredness and moxie that steered me throughout my twenties and thirties, building up my advertising and editorial careers, propelling me to far-flung corners of the world, seemed to have abandoned me. I had identified myself as an independent woman for so long, rarely giving in to self-doubt or questioning what I was doing, where I was going, when things would happen to me, or why I made the choices I did. But suddenly, I was analyzing everything. My fortieth birthday loomed, sparking questions I had long put to bed: Where was I going? What was important to me? What was my idea of success? I felt compelled to figure out "life"—as if it were something I could do on an afternoon stroll along the Hudson River.

Part of my angst was that my book launch was now well behind me. The years leading up to its publication and the months celebrating its debut were over, leaving a hole in my life. Something that had percolated inside my brain and that I had obsessed about for years was gone, and I didn't know where to funnel all that creative energy. It was like I had a phantom limb; I always felt like there was something I should be doing or writing…but what? It was disorienting no longer having a sense of purpose or urgency.

The other part was my job. Ever since joining the ad industry as an eager twenty-two-year-old, I've had a pretty good run. Inspiring bosses, collaborative teams, work that I was proud of—some that had even won awards. I considered myself lucky to have a relatively cushy job like advertising. Even if of questionable ethics, it's a young, fun industry, and educational to boot. I've gone to BMW driving school, learned how to scale walls at YMCA day camp, and seen how sweet potatoes are pulverized into baby food and how leather hides are transformed into handbags worth several months' rent.

When I came back from Paris with Louis Vuitton dominating my portfolio, a whole new world of fashion and luxury advertising was open to me, and I jumped right in. Talk about being seduced by all the wrong things. This downtown boutique agency I had joined about nine months after my return to New York was nothing like the larger, more established ones I was used to. And while those previous jobs were occasionally blighted by office politics and drama, none of it came close to the dysfunction I was experiencing now. This agency was firmly divided between the cool kids and everyone else. I was not one of the cool kids. Nearly twenty years into my career, suddenly I couldn't get anything right. I didn't dress right, talk right, or know the right people. Judging by how diminished my role was, apparently I couldn't even write right.

The whole atmosphere started wearing me down, especially Dennis, the executive creative director. He was advertising's worst cliché of a moody, egomaniacal tyrant. He was supposed to be an inspiring leader, overseeing and fostering the talent within the creative department, but he really didn't want anything to do with any of us—he just liked having minions to lord over and be witness to his daily genius. He was incredibly talented, but he was also deeply troubled. Not just capricious, but clinical. In the year I'd been there, he'd churned through four assistants and chewed out everyone in the department. His freak-outs were legendary: the way he'd rant and rave, pacing around the lofty, sunlit room filled with art and fashion tomes, spit flying from his lips, hands waving madly in the air, screaming and moaning about some idiot client or worthless employee or asinine decision. As he did, everyone's IM would light up, with all of us stifling giggles, eyes popping in disbelief over his dramatic displays and lack of empathy. It was just so ridiculous—unless you were the target of his wrath. Then, it was no laughing matter.

My turn came soon enough. I was briefed at the very last minute to come up with a campaign line that was better than the one a client had already suggested. I had shared a couple dozen options with Dennis the previous day, which he vaguely responded to, neither accepting nor rejecting, as was his style. As noncommunicative as he could be, he was the kind of person whose body language is quite clear. I knew my lines hadn't passed muster not because of something so direct and obvious as a "None of these are working; try again," but because he insisted he was too busy to meet me the rest of the day. Whenever I'd try, he was occupied indeed—looking at magazines, talking on the phone, or hanging out with his select sidekicks who were always on standby to stroke his ego. His assistant simply couldn't fit me in. So I worked late on more lines and came in early the next day, when I knew there would be no shields or distractions. I walked over to the table where he sat alone, sorting through reams of scrap images, preparing for a presentation. "Morning—"

"Amy, you didn't do it. Just forget it," he said coldly, giving me but a brief look of disgust.

"But I have some new lines—"

"Just…get out of my face," he said emotionlessly, continuing to sift through his images, glasses perched on the tip of his nose, his warm, cozy cashmere sweater belying the cold heart beneath. With his sneer and obvious disdain, I knew I should walk away. Yet I found myself standing there. As masochistic as it was, I *wanted* him to pace and scream and let his torrent loose. At least that was behavior I was accustomed to and knew it wasn't personal, it was just *him*. But the little dismissive wave of his hand he gave indicating that he couldn't even be bothered cut through my thin veneer of confidence. Not only had I failed at coming up with the perfect line, but I was also failing to have any sort of meaningful relationship or satisfying project at this agency. It's one thing to have a bad day or a crummy boss, but never feeling good enough was taking its toll. I returned to my crappy, little cubicle within the grand loft, grateful that no one was in the office yet to witness that belittling moment but shamefaced nonetheless. I felt conspicuous and superfluous. My self-esteem was eroding by the week. I had to get out of there.

Things quickly went from bad to worse when another writer joined the agency. This should have been a good thing, as the workload had been building and I needed support for the shitstorm that had become my day-to-day existence. But this writer brought a whole other level of insanity.

Her name was Heidi, and she arrived at the office on a Monday morning and, within a week, fell into an awe-inspiring routine. She'd saunter in, all five feet ten inches, fair skin, bleached hair, and black sunglasses—occasionally as early as ten, but usually between ten thirty and eleven. Once she was situated, she would bust out a mirror and start putting on her makeup. Then, once she had her face on, she would casually mention she had to pop out for an errand and come back with a giant sandwich from the bodega and proceed to chomp down. By the time noon rolled around, she might be ready to work.

"Heidi, you're amazing! You just blow my mind," Dennis announced two weeks into her tenure, loud enough to ensure all of us in the creative department could hear him. She was such a slacker, a mixture of overconfidence and incompetence, and yet in Dennis's eyes, she was the second coming. "This! Copy! Is! Brilliant!" he moaned pleasurably about whatever she had written for some overpriced designer jeans. I could sense everyone's intrigue about the new girl—for it wasn't every day that Dennis dispensed such orgasmic praise—and their pity for me, the old one. Heidi let out an awkward guffaw in the cube next to me, relishing the spotlight, while I sank lower in my seat.

By now, I felt like a true loser. I was being out-written by someone fifteen years my junior. Even worse, I sadly realized I used to be that girl. The ingénue. The one creative directors gushed about. The one with nothing but opportunity and possibility ahead of me. Now I was a worthless, uninspired, middle-aged hack.

"Aren't you supposed to become *more* confident as you get older?" I asked AJ over the phone. A few years ago, we would have been bellied up at a bar together, sipping prosecco, or eating cupcakes at Billy's Bakery, enveloped in the comforting baking smells. But two years after having their baby, AJ and Mitchell had left the city. It was inevitable that our days of carousing would come to a close, but sporadic phone calls between naptimes and office hours just didn't have the same satisfaction for the soul as our tête-à-têtes. "I swear, I can feel the insecurity creeping into my bones. Pretty soon, it's going to take over and shut me down," I told her, clearly being none too dramatic. But I felt safe with AJ. In high school, we talked on the phone every afternoon. She understood where I came from and who I was. She'd seen me through breakups, layoffs, all-nighters, hangovers, crying fits, jealousy streaks—she championed me, even in my worst moments. She also knew me to be fearless, creative, and outspoken. Maybe she could tell me where I was going wrong with Dennis and Heidi.

"Aim, you need to get out of there. You know you're an

amazing writer, and you've always had great relationships with your bosses. I mean, it's not you—this guy is just crazy." I could hear the mixture of sympathy and anger in her voice.

"I know, he's batshit crazy," I admitted. "But I feel so beaten down. I've been talking to a headhunter, but I don't even know if I can get excited about going to another agency and doing the same thing somewhere else."

"But don't you think it will be different somewhere else? Somewhere where the people are nice and sane? You owe it to yourself to just get out of there."

I sighed. I appreciated her optimism and support—I needed it. Yet as much as I wanted to leave this job, I was paralyzed. I was worried that Dennis was right: What if my talent had dried up? What if I just wasn't a good writer? What if my ad days were over? What if I was forty and stuck in a career that overpaid me but undermined my confidence? I felt so low, yet I didn't know if I had the strength to leave.

AJ and I went through my options: I could go freelance, but then I'd have to pay out-of-pocket for insurance, which would eat up most of the money I'd have to hustle to make, if I were lucky enough to get steady gigs. I could try breaking into a magazine to pursue my passion as a food and travel writer full-time, but I'd probably have to start at the bottom, as an assistant—a forty-year-old assistant. I could open that candy store I had always fantasized about—something magical like Miette in San Francisco, where I'd feel happy every day just being surrounded by brightly patterned chocolate bars and pretty cakes fit for society's best. But that would entail hijacking all the savings, and then some, that was earmarked for our apartment down payment. I could just quit for the satisfaction of it—God, that would feel good—but I was admittedly wearing golden handcuffs. I may have been miserable, but I also couldn't imagine severing myself from my generous semimonthly paycheck, paid vacation time, and health benefits that included nearly 100% coverage of my beloved therapist—though ironically, most of my time with her was now spent with me agonizing over this job and her strategizing about how to get me out of it. AJ and I turned over all the options, but at the end of our call, we came to the same conclusion we had five, ten, even twenty years ago: getting old sucks.

So yeah, somewhere between the highs of being in love and the lows triggered by my job, I turned forty. By now, Andrew knew that the way to my heart was through food, and he made reservations for the momentous occasion at one of the most epic spots, not just in the city, but in the whole world: Eleven Madison Park.

The restaurant's elegant art deco interior—all refined elegance with its 30-foot ceilings, gold leaf ceiling and rich leather banquettes—is tucked inside the landmark Met Life building on the edge of Madison Square Park. It was founded in 1998 by Danny Meyer, probably the city's friendliest, most hospitable, and most successful restaurateur. Meyer is responsible for restaurants like Gramercy Tavern and Union Square Café, which have become institutions that define classic New York dining. These restaurants prove that Meyer has a Midas touch. He understands the essential balance of atmosphere, hospitality, menu and food. He intuits customer needs as well as dining trends. Whether high or low (Have you heard of Shake Shack? That's Meyer's creation too), he puts incredible consideration into everything, and the result-ing quality can't be beat.

With Eleven Madison Park, he made perhaps his best decision in 2006 when he hired Chef Daniel Humm from Campton Place in San Francisco. The Swiss-born chef, the youngest in his country's history to earn a Michelin star at the age of twenty-four, was both classically trained and wildly inventive. Shortly after arriving at Eleven Madison Park, Daniel pushed for a new general manager who could bring equal passion and innovation to the front of the house, which he felt the restaurant needed. Meyer suggested Will Guidara.

At the time, Will was only twenty-six and running Meyer's two cafés at the Museum of Modern Art. When approached with this new opportunity, he wasn't terribly keen to move from the informal cafés to fine dining, which is notoriously stuffy. But he was persuaded to at least speak with Daniel, and in doing so, he found a kindred spirit. Will and Daniel shared histories of growing up in the restaurant world. They were both extremely dedicated to their professions and planned to eventually run their own restaurants. After hours of conversation and consideration, they realized it would be more fun if they pursued their ambitions together. Will came aboard Eleven Madison Park.

It didn't take long for the pair to find their magic. The restaurant soon had three stars from the *New York Times* and Michelin, James Beard Awards, plus a spot on San Pellegrino's World's 50 Best Restaurants awards. Even so, they hungered for more and strategized about how to make it happen. "As Eleven Madison Park evolved, we were feeling a couple things really powerfully," Will remembers. Crucially, they realized that the most energy happened when a dish was brought to the middle of the table, instead of each individual diner receiving a plate. When something was shared and communal, it sparked a more special and memorable dynamic. This prompted them to move exclusively to a tasting menu—a practical but poetic decision. "Within the tasting menu," Will says, "you have this ability to tell a story with more of an orchestrated narrative than you do with shorter menus." After this move, the restaurant continued to rise with the *New York Times* bumping them from three to four stars and they ascended to number twenty-four on the World's 50 Best Restaurants.

One of the great things about owning your own restaurant—for the ambitious duo bought Eleven Madison Park from Danny Meyer in 2011—is that you can travel the world, eating at restaurants in the name of research and inspiration. As Will and Daniel did so, traveling from Piedmont to Tokyo to Lyon, they had another important revelation: their most memorable experiences were those that were authentic to the location. Inspired by this awareness, they looked to their home city and evolved the tasting menu. "We wanted to craft an experience centered around New York, something that wouldn't make sense anywhere else in the world," Will said, adding, "We felt our city deserved that." This focus on iconic dishes and local ingredients was the tasting menu that Andrew and I shared.

When they launched their new tasting menu, some people thought the theme was sentimental and gimmicky. I couldn't have been more delighted to celebrate my love for my city along with my milestone birthday. For four hours, Andrew and I were presented with course after course of delightful creations, imaginative pairings, and, always, dramatic presentations. Little fillets of sturgeon arrived under a glass dome, after which it was lifted, applewood smoke billowed out across the table. Pretzel bread, cheese, and ale, meant to evoke a picnic in Central Park, was delivered in a picnic basket. But my favorite dish was the carrot tartare.

The idea came, along with many of the menu's other

courses, while researching and reflecting upon New York's iconic restaurants. From 21 Club to Four Seasons, once upon a time, every establishment offered a signature steak tartare. "'What's *our* tartare?'" Will and Daniel wondered. They kept playing with formulas and recipes and coming close to something special, but it never quite had the wow factor they were looking for. One day after Daniel returned from Paffenroth Gardens, a farm in the Hudson Valley with rich muck soil that yields incredibly flavorful root vegetables, they had a moment. "In his perfect Swiss accent, he said, 'What about if we used carrots?'" Will remembers. And so the carrot tartare, a sublime ode to the humble vegetable, was added to the Eleven Madison Park tasting course.

"I love that moment when you clamp a meat grinder onto the table and people expect it to be meat, and it's not," Will gushes of the theatrical tableside presentation. After the vibrant carrots are ground by the server, they're turned over to you along with a palette of ingredients with which to mix and play: pickled mustard seeds, quail egg yolk, pea mustard, smoked bluefish, spicy vinaigrette. It was one of the most enlightening yet simple dishes I've ever had. I didn't know exactly which combination of ingredients I mixed, adding a little of this and a little of that, but every bite I created was fresh, bright, and ringing with flavor. Carrots—who knew?

Dinner carried on. The courses transitioned to dessert. Midnight approached. I sat back in the beautiful corner table we had been bequeathed for the night, considering the magnificent dining room that had emptied of most other diners. Every course we shared had indeed brought Andrew and I together in the moment. I knew this meal was something I'd remember for years. As we were sent out into the night with a handwritten birthday note, homemade granola for the next morning, and warm good nights from the staff, I was beyond satisfied. I was enamored. Maybe forty wouldn't be so bad after all.

Some women treat themselves to fancy jewelry for their birthdays. Or a day at the spa. Or at least a blow-out. I took a trip to the fertility clinic.

Having been single for so long, I had hedged my bets about kids and figured, quite practically, that they might not be in my future. Throughout my thirties, I reasoned it would take meeting someone who knocked my socks off and us both wanting to try to start a family and then having the stars and fates align before I had to give it any serious consideration. I knew a nontraditional path to love and motherhood—perhaps marrying in my fifties and adopting a child then, whether I remained single or had a partner—was likely. Well, I had now met someone who knocked my socks off. Should we start a family? Was it in the stars?

Andrew had also been single for a long time and shared the same unhurried perspective. We had casually talked about children in the year we had been together and agreed they would be a "nice to have"—something that might happen down the road. When we talked about it, we used the same hypothetical tone. But I was forty now. As you get older, the likelihood of conceiving continuously declines, while the chances of complications go up. Thirty-five is when everyone—single women, their overeager relatives, and random opinionated strangers alike—typically starts clucking. Forty is when you're really doomed. If kids were going to be part of my and Andrew's future, I could no longer afford a laissez-faire attitude.

I kept thinking of a conversation I'd had with Mel several months ago. She had seen me through a health scare back when I lived in Paris, when I had ovarian cysts and didn't know what it meant for my reproductive future. When she knew things with Andrew were turning serious, she didn't just encourage me to try; she insisted. "If you think there's even a shred of a possibility that you want kids, then go for it," she said in a way that might have felt irksome or overbearing if had been anyone else. But Mel has been through so many similar health and emotional experiences as me, it's like I'm walking in her experienced, enlightened footsteps. She is a special spirit sister and I trust her guidance implicitly. "Do not wait. Do not have any regrets," she had said. And I knew she was right.

Clearly, from my recent angst, turning forty wasn't so great for my psychic energy, but what did it mean for my ovaries? What were my chances of getting pregnant if I were to go off the pill? What were my options if I couldn't? When would I know to intervene with a treatment, and, given I was already behind the eight ball, was it better to jump right in with fertility drugs? These were my questions as I sat with another middle-aged woman, this one a smartly dressed doctor, inside the Midtown office of a gigantic fertility clinic. She had questions for me too, so I shared my entire biological history, including inauspicious events like a tumor on my pituitary gland as a teenager, a lifetime of irregular periods, and those cysts I'd had on my ovaries just a few years prior. Putting those things on the table along with my age, I figured my likelihood of getting pregnant was slim at best, but I was surprised to hear her tell me that I'd have a 20 percent chance each month. "Twenty percent until proven otherwise," she noted. Once she had my history jotted down, she went into my options in what seemed ascending cost, complication, and commitment.

First up: blood work and an ultrasound. The number and viability of eggs decrease with age, and these basic tests would give us the general state of my uterus and ovaries. The next test, a hysterosalpingogram (HSG), would ensure my fallopian tubes, the gateway between the ovaries and uterus, were open and therefore able to receive sperm. Speaking of,

Andrew would have to be tested too. Assuming everything thus far was checking out, we'd want to be strategic about having sex, using an ovulation kit to know when I was ovulating. "Not the electronic ones," the doctor emphasized. "The one with the smiley face." If all of that checked out, and I wasn't getting pregnant after a few months, then we could start looking at fertility treatments. That could mean taking pills to induce ovulation or getting shots in the butt, like a few of my friends had done (you don't get to be a forty-year-old woman without having friends who have endured one fertility treatment or another). Then came intrauterine insemination (IUI), or when sperm is "cleaned" in the lab and then inserted directly into the uterus, giving it a better chance to connect with an egg. The last option before things got too sci-fi was in vitro fertilization (IVF), when mature eggs are collected from your ovaries and put together with the sperm in the lab, and then reinserted in your uterus if and when any of the egg(s) became fertilized. It was a whole new world to understand and consider.

"Go off the pill for starters," the doctor advised. "It will take a couple cycles to begin ovulating again. Then we can take it from there. There's no need to decide now what you want to do. Give it some thought."

Indeed, she had given me plenty to think about. More important, she had given me hope. The doctor had been, if not optimistic, at least reassuring. It really seemed like getting pregnant as a forty-year-old was a possibility. Yet I left the office with an unsettled feeling in the pit of my stomach: I still had to tell Andrew that I wanted to go off the pill.

I wasted no time. That Saturday night, Andrew and I decided to stay in rather than duke it out at a hot new restaurant where we'd inevitably be relegated to the bar for forty minutes past our reservation time by a control-happy hostess, all the while being jostled by a fleet of irritated servers who couldn't get through with their plates of sea urchin and offal for the mildly drunk and rowdy diners screaming across their tables while also drowning in rock music. I guess you could say I was finding the city's restaurant scene less charming than I used to. Andrew cooked instead.

We sat bohemian style on the floor at his coffee table, bread crumbs and wine rings littering the surface. Ryan Adams, Wilco, and Lucinda Williams shuffled through the speakers. Andrew had made one of his few but impressive signature dishes: tomato soup that's so laden with peasant bread that it probably has more carbs than Sicilian pizza.

"So, you know how we've talked about kids and agreed that maybe someday it would be nice to have them?" I asked, dropping this out-of-the-blue question as nonchalantly as possible.

Andrew smiled and rolled with it, "Yeah."

"And you know how I just turned forty?" I soldiered on. Still smiling, Andrew responded, "Yeah."

"Well." I paused, nervous that my going to the clinic without his knowledge might sound like I was plotting to go off and have a brood of kids regardless of whether he was on board. Andrew was the priority here, but I had felt responsible to know the current state of my childbearing capabilities before raising the topic. "Well," I started again, "I got a referral to a fertility specialist from my ob-gyn, and I went." Andrew's eyebrows shot up, but he continued eating his soup without any other signs of alarm. "Basically—and I just went for information, I didn't get any tests or anything," I told him. "But she said the first and most obvious step, if I do—if *we* do want to get pregnant, is to go off the pill."

Andrew put his spoon down and listened attentively, as I shared all that the doctor had explained to me. "I'm still not even one hundred percent sure—we have so much other stuff going on right now—but I wanted to at least know what our options are," I explained to him. "Because I feel like even though we *haven't* spent a ton of time talking about it, and we've both said we'd be okay if we *didn't* have kids, I *do* think we should give it a chance. We should at least *try*." He was looking at me with such love. I don't know why I was so surprised. "Right? Don't you think we should at least *try* to get pregnant? I think I should go off the pill."

There. It was out there. No matter how Andrew responded,

no matter what happened from here, I had spoken my mind and put it out in the universe. After forty years, I had acknowledged that I wanted and was ready to have kids. Andrew leaned across the table and kissed me. "Babe, we're going to have an incredible life no matter what," he said. "But I agree, let's go for it. Let's try to have a baby!"

It was the simplest response to one of the biggest decisions I had made in my life. And with it, I was reminded again that Andrew was the right one for me.

DOABLE
DECADENCE

Eleven Madison Park enjoys status as one of only six New York restaurants with three Michelin stars (Per Se, Jean-Georges, Masa, Le Bernadin, and Chef's Table at Brooklyn Fare are the others). At any of these establishments, you can expect a consistent level of mind-blowing pomp and presentation. When you start exploring one-Michelin-starred restaurants, the list becomes a bit more eclectic—perfect for a celebratory night out.

A "Parisian steakhouse meets classic New York City tavern," Keith McNally's Minetta Tavern in the West Village is a gem. Dark and old-timey, filled with history and clamoring with mature hipsters, it fits the bill for a buzzy night out.

Rebelle, located on the Bowery, reminds me a lot of the current restaurants being born in Paris. Slick, modern, slightly austere, and as inventive with its menu as it is progressive with its wine program, it's a sophisticated standout that somehow still feels undiscovered.

With its smart interior design and offbeat vibe, the Musket Room really feels like it could be in New Zealand—where the Nolita restaurant's chef and co-owner hails from. It's cozy and casual despite its elegant plating of the Kiwi-influenced menu.

A Korean-Italian mash-up, Piora is a small, dignified, unexpected delight in the West Village. Its pristine dining room and back garden make it the perfect setting for a special night.

CHAPTER 5

The Perfect Home (Fries)

So the race began. Not the baby-making race, though we were devoted to that mission too, but the great hunt for a Brooklyn apartment.

"Check all the boxes off your wish list! This lofty and light two bedroom, two bath boasts hardwood floors, seamless flow, and a generous private—*all caps*," Andrew noted, "outdoor space." He was reading the *New York Times* real estate listings aloud, having fun with the broker lingo, which had become all too familiar to us. When we agreed several months earlier to put off our apartment search until we felt more ready to live together, we had no idea we'd be pushing ourselves into one of the tightest housing markets in history. Since the start of the New Year, prices were going up weekly, and we had already been outbid three times in six weeks. As the media and real estate brokers now loved to say, "Brooklyn is the new New York."

The borough's booming popularity combined with record low mortgage rates and inventory, a hangover effect from the 2008 financial crash when all new construction halted, meant slim pickings. Every Sunday morning, we woke up and culled a list of the day's most-promising open houses from the real estate listings. Whereas we could once find four, five, sometimes six apartments to look at in a day, now we were lucky to see three. Even if we had doubts, we went to look at a place in person. It wasn't that desperation was setting in—or come to think of it, yes, it was—but we were also starting to second-guess ourselves. Maybe we *could* learn to love loft living. Maybe all subterranean apartments *weren't* dark and depressing. The hunt was becoming a test of patience and endurance. Andrew went on, "Pet friendly, elevator building, on-premise fitness center..."

"How big is it?" I asked, running through my mental checklist of must-haves. So many of these two-bedroom listings were bogus, with the second bedroom barely large enough to fit a crib or dresser, much less both. Last weekend, we had actually seen a place in Park Slope—the epicenter of trendy parenting, which made me not want to live there if only I could afford to be so picky—where the baby's bedroom was the parent's walk-in closet. Despite the increasing odds of finding an affordable two-bedroom apartment, we couldn't let our enthusiasm wane. I was officially off the pill so an actual second bedroom for our as-of-yet conceived baby was a must. We needed a fight song to psyche us up—like "Eye of the Tiger." *Dant! Dant-dant-dant! Dant-dant-daaaaaaant!*

As we sat on Andrew's mid-century couch developing the day's open-house itinerary, I found myself also creating a mental inventory of his belongings. Not only was I nervous about living with someone again—it had been a decade since I had accommodated anyone else's rhythms and routines—but I was starting to freak out about consolidating our furniture and deciding whose coffee table, duvet cover, and kitchen knives would get the boot. I'm a sentimentalist; I don't readily part with things. But I knew it was time to practice my partnership skills.

"Let's see...975-square-feet," he said, glancing up at me through his glasses, looking like Mark Ruffalo, the perfect blend of sweet and sexy.

"Hmmm, below the thousand-square-foot threshold. Does it say anything about closet space?" Another apartment must-have for any New Yorker: deep closets to stash such essentials as off-season clothing, old tax files, and the collection of chocolate and macaron boxes one accrues in life.

"It doesn't say. But there's a tax abatement. That's good— the maintenance is low."

"Let me see the layout," I said, angling his iPhone so I

could scope the closet situation and see this "seamless flow" the listing promised.

"Meh. Not awesome, but we should probably check it out," I concluded, putting my head on his shoulder.

When you're watching your fifth straight hour of *House Hunters* on HGTV or drooling over a stack of *ELLE Decor*s, the concept of "real estate porn" is all kinds of sexy. So much square footage to fantasize about, so many charming details to moan about, nothing but glossy Technicolor possibility. But when you're actually in the market to buy something, and you are bound by a timeline and a budget, and the pickings are slim, practicality, not porn, is on your mind. The initial high I got from these open-house marathons was long gone and at the end of Sunday afternoons, I now felt physically and emotionally wasted.

"That's about it, babe." Andrew snapped his phone off, leaning over to put his arm around me and peer at the pad where I had written down four prospects and organized our route according to the addresses and times of the open houses. The fun part of this weekly plotting was deciding which neighborhood bakery we'd try or what new restaurant we could brunch at given our particular circuit. In Dumbo, we'd trek through the cobblestone streets to reach Vinegar Hill House and their plate-sized sourdough pancake. Park Slope always warranted a visit to Blue Sky Bakery, where there was always something warm from the oven off their rotating menu of deliciously off-kilter flavors like banana-chocolate bran, apple walnut pumpkin, and triple berry—if you got there early enough. And even though we weren't looking to move to Red Hook, so remote and removed as it was from any public transportation, we were persuaded to visit more than one open house in the vicinity just to brunch at HOME/MADE, a tiny bohemian joint that had the best scrambles and home fries in the city, served with fat slabs of Balthazar walnut bread, buttered and grilled to perfection.

The backdrop of hardscrabble Red Hook couldn't be more appropriate for the tale of HOME/MADE and the two women who have battled against fires and hurricanes, disputed leases and anemic foot traffic, to keep the restaurant alive. Their story began in the wake of 9/11, when Monica Byrne, a born-and-raised New Yorker, returned from San Francisco, where she had been running a restaurant in Ghirardelli Square. After the World Trade Center tragedy, she felt compelled to be back home, but she had no job. While looking for a new gig, the owner of a bar in Red Hook, located on a protrusion off the southern tip of Brooklyn that has a history pockmarked with poverty and crime, asked if she'd be interested in running the kitchen. She was.

While working there, Monica fell in love with the

neighborhood and its gritty, artistic sensibility. She kept day-dreaming about opening her own small wine bar where she could import a California vibe to accompany a simple, seasonal cuisine and give the locals an upscale alternative to the plethora of neighborhood dive bars. "I wanted a nice, clean space where you could come by yourself and not have to worry about being hit on," she explained. And so Tini was born: a wee spot for wine and cheese that was like being in someone's small but chic living room. Monica opened it with her partner Leisah Swenson, but it was short lived, partly because the neighborhood wasn't ready for something so "fancy" and partly because they had lease issues that forced them out of the space. Fortunately, another spot down Van Brunt, the main drag of Red Hook, was available and the women decided to hit the restart button, moving and expanding their business.

HOME/MADE, Monica and Leisah's new restaurant, opened in the spring of 2009 and yet, despite the stellar cooking, the business was constantly tried. "It's Red Hook; there are not a lot of walk-ins," Monica explained of the short-lived artisanal soup-and-salad lunch service. Then they had a fire, which set them back financially, forcing them to reevaluate hours and offerings. And then the sucker punch came in October of 2012 by the name of Hurricane Sandy. A historic storm, Sandy put the entire neighborhood under water. Despite pledges, government assistance never came through, and the massive flooding sustained by the neighborhood's small businesses took its toll, including HOME/MADE. Monica and Leisah couldn't afford the operating costs, staffing, and supplies afterward, so they terminated dinner service and doubled downed on their catering business and their most popular service: brunch. "It's the one thing people come all over for," Monica says.

Andrew and I had our first HOME/MADE brunch with AJ, Mitchell, Ben, and Merrill, sitting in the pebbled backyard on wooden benches made wavy by years of being outside. Forever a sweet freak, I ordered the french toast, an enormous square of brioche smothered under a compote of fruit that was utterly divine. But it was Andrew's scramble that made us devoted repeat visitors to HOME/MADE.

Every once in a while at a restaurant, the dish you order looks so good, you don't even know where to begin tackling it. Such are HOME/MADE's scrambles. There are four simple options—my favorite is the smoked salmon, goat cheese, and dill—along with the occasional special or seasonal flavor, and they're served with soft, savory home fries and slabs of grilled walnut bread. Let's break it down:

The scramble: Monica, who doesn't even like eggs, created these sublime scrambles with a specific and studied technique. "We whisk the hell out of them," she says, ticking off her methodology on her fingers. "We use cream, not milk. And we keep turning them and turning them until they're fluffy and in one piece, not broken into bits of egg."

The toast: While the rave worthiness of toast usually boils down to the quality of the bread, HOME/MADE takes it a step further. "The flame char is my happiness," the chef explains of her preference for grilling bread instead of toasting it, as 99 percent of restaurants do. That it's walnut bread from Balthazar, one of the city's best French bakeries, doesn't hurt.

The home fries, or roasted potatoes as Monica insists on calling them, abiding by chefs' definitions of home fries (small fried chunks of potatoes) versus hash browns (shredded potatoes fried greasy on the griddle) versus roasted potatoes (roasted in the oven instead of fried on the stovetop): "My potatoes I've been making for a hundred years," she says with a smile (really, it's been about twenty). The recipe came when she was roasting potatoes early on in her career and thought they were too bland. She didn't want to just keep adding salt so instead she reached for the mustard, which her mom always used on fries. "It just was everything," she says of the tangy, vinegary flavor the French condiment lent to her spuds. Along with the new potatoes, mustard, and herbs de Provence, she uses whole jacket garlic cloves in the roasting pan. It's a simple recipe that's also "a Zen exercise," as the potatoes have to be continuously turned every fifteen minutes to get them hard and crispy on the outside and soft and billowy on the inside.

They're perfect. The perfect home fries. Or roasted potatoes...whatever you want to call them. But a couple months into our apartment search, I just wanted to call something home.

As Andrew and I navigated the open houses in the wintery slush and biting wind, it wasn't just the elements we were battling. It wasn't just the tight market. It was all those couples with their skinny jeans, plaid Steven Alan shirts, and determined attitudes descending from Manhattan. They were so annoying. So predictable. They were so…like us.

Here I had been thinking that Andrew and I were unique in our desire to shack up together in Brooklyn. But we were quickly discovering that every other middle-age-ish, professional couple—many already sporting BabyBjörns and UPPAbaby strollers, the de rigueur urban parenting gear—was also searching for a two-bedroom, two-bath apartment in Brooklyn. In fact, we were a dime a dozen. The more we made these open-house circuits, devoting Sundays to the search for a new home, determined to be part of the great Brooklyn migration, the more the self-loathing kicked in.

At first the open houses were like going to a friend's friend's singles mixer—the apartment would be filled with people who were vaguely familiar, like you'd probably met before. There was polite camaraderie as we discreetly checked each other out, sizing up the competition and making the most of our shared situation. But then the market heated up so much that lines started forming down the borough's coveted brownstone stoops just to get into the open houses. Any notion of politesse went out the window as, two by two, we crammed inside the apartments to the point of claustrophobia. Everyone gave each other the stink eye, while stealthily confirming that the kitchen had stainless steel and commercial-grade appliances, and sniffing out bonus amenities like stackable washer-dryers, walk-in pantries, and wine refrigerators. We all stubbornly held our ground, trying in vain to appear nonchalant as we whipped out tape measures to see what size bed could fit in the second bedroom or tried to obstruct every other attendee's view of the decorative fireplace in the master bedroom—anything to discourage a competing bid, which would wipe out our offer and put us back to square one.

Inevitably, tensions flared; everyone was as frustrated by the scene as we were, getting snippy and territorial. Some guy called Andrew an asshole when Andrew neglected to hold the apartment door open for him as we were leaving and he was arriving. If the search had ever been fun and full of promise, it was no longer. It was a first world problem, but bleakness was setting in. My faith in mankind was evaporating. Were we ever going to live together? Would the real estate gods come to smile upon us? Would Brooklyn ever be home?

Truman Capote once said, "I live in Brooklyn, by choice." He was not alone. Tons of bright personalities have proudly called Brooklyn their home: Walt Whitman and Jonathan Lethem, Norman Mailer and Nathan Englander, Betty Smith and Myla Goldberg, Adam Yauch and Jay Z, Spike Lee and Marisa Tomei, and let's not forget Miranda's ultimate move to the outer borough. What is it about the sprawling borough that's been the siren's call for so long?

In 1898, Brooklyn was its own city—the fourth largest in the nation. Then, consolidation happened. Along with Queens, the Bronx, and Staten Island, Brooklyn was engulfed by Manhattan, creating New York City as we know it. For decades, Brooklyn remained in the shadow of Manhattan, forever the ugly stepchild. It became radically diverse, home to Russians, Poles, Hasidic Jews, Dominicans, Italians, Africans, and dozens of other minority groups. But every year since the turn of the millennium, Brooklyn has become more and more of an international destination and, in the process, a brand. Parisians especially love Brooklyn, declaring anything with certain rustic coolness as "*très* Brooklyn." As the borough has gentrified, it's become deified as well as the object of scorn, what with its artisanal pickle makers, craft beer brewers, and vegan soap makers.

And now, as we were sadly discovering with the booming

real estate market, there was a whole new movement afoot. Brooklyn wasn't just for creative types and artistic spirits; it was for bourgeois breeders. The price of apartments was going up before our very eyes, making us worried that we'd be priced right out of the market. We realized our initial focus on Brooklyn Heights, Cobble Hill, and Boerum Hill— three quintessential Brooklyn neighborhoods with bucolic street names like Pineapple and Willow—would have to be expanded. So we started looking in Carroll Gardens, Prospect Heights, and Fort Greene, each a little more remote but still thriving with indie boutiques, organic coffeehouses, and mom-and-pop restaurants. Then we contemplated going still deeper into the borough, to less gentrified and glorified neighborhoods. We hiked to the desolate Gowanus Canal but didn't share the Elsen sisters' affinity for it; along Fort Greene's Myrtle Avenue, nicknamed "Murder Avenue" as it was home to some of the most infamous housing projects; and tried to ignore the highway traffic spilling into South Slope. Each time we expanded our range, we nervously recalculated the commute into Manhattan and reconsidered our must-haves. Were we willing to give up laundry inside the unit for a subway stop on the corner? Could we handle hauling groceries up to a fourth-floor walk-up or the potential rodent invasion of a subterranean apartment? Was a second bedroom that could fit a crib but not a dresser a deal breaker after all?

Sunday after Sunday, we were ninja-like, canvassing the borough, ducking in and out of open houses. We had seen dozens of options. There was the L-shaped charmer in Carroll Gardens with an open kitchen and working fireplace, the new condo on Fourth Avenue with a balcony overlooking the Statue of Liberty and downtown Manhattan, a converted schoolhouse in Prospect Heights, and an old factory along the "Columbia Waterfront District"—real estate brokers' neologism for the remote strip between Red Hook and Cobble Hill. There was the new Dumbo building that was already being sued by its occupants for shoddy construction, the depressing garden unit that rattled from traffic on the nearby BQE, and the second-floor apartment so close to the new Barclays Center—home to the Brooklyn Nets, traveling circuses, and teenybopper concerts—that was virtually like living in the middle of the busy five-way intersection. We saw narrow railroad apartments where we could hold hands and touch opposite sides of the room, triangle-shaped bedrooms, and floors that sloped at fifteen-degree angles. We wept with desire for all the beautifully remodeled brownstones with double parlors, twelve-foot ceilings, and pocket doors, and cried in disbelief at all the dubious condos, erected as if overnight for this rush of buyers. In the middle of it all, more affordable apartments were surfacing in Manhattan, so we started going to open houses there, ready to give up on the Brooklyn dream.

We saw it all, and we bid like Russian oligarchs at a Sotheby's auction, as if money were no object. Who did we think we were? We were delusional by then, carried away by the frenzy. The reality was, we were willing to pay hundreds of thousands of dollars for an apartment that we not only didn't love, that not only didn't tick all the boxes of our search criteria, but that we had also spent all of seven or eight minutes superficially perusing in a sea of people. Our future home, our life savings—a whim. If we stopped to think about it, it was insane. But we couldn't stop to think about it. We didn't have time. We couldn't afford to. If we did, we could lose out on our slim chance of scoring a Brooklyn apartment.

Our wake-up call came when we finally had an offer accepted on a three-bedroom apartment with a glorious living room, lined with built-in bookshelves and full of natural light. I had visions of stretching out on the floor there every Sunday morning with the paper while Andrew recreated HOME/MADE's scrambles and home fries in the open kitchen. Andrew and I were on a high for days after our broker called with the news, reveling in the fact that we had finally beat the market and gotten this place, a *three*-bedroom no less. Then, one night as we were eating sundaes at the bar of DBGB for an article I was writing, Andrew casually mentioned our future home's second-floor location. An alarm went off in my head. My very first apartment in Manhattan was on the second floor, and suddenly I remembered every pigeon coo and penny drop I had ever heard while living there. We asked our broker for a second viewing of the apartment, so we could be there without the throngs of open-house attendees and just listen.

We arrived on a weekday evening and sheepishly realized it was not only on the second floor, but it also faced Flatbush Avenue, one of the busiest throughways in the borough, ushering rideshare vans, public buses, and anxious commuters from the Manhattan Bridge to East Brooklyn. I stood in the window watching the traffic and got to see what our view would be: a Chase bank with neon blue signage, a twenty-four-hour, florescent-lit Duane Reade, and a billboard, currently promoting Z100. The smell of Tex-Mex from the greasy takeout joint below might counteract the bus fumes, but there was no way of getting around the work the apartment itself needed. The kitchen and two bathrooms, circa 1979 judging by the pink tile and brass fixtures, needed to be gut renovated. Two of the three bedrooms—which were side by side, neither of which had a closet—were so tiny and bizarrely shaped, we'd have to tear down the wall between them to make the space functional. Lastly, we'd have to install new floors throughout or live with the industrial carpeting that looked as though it had been there since the days of *Three's Company*. Right there and then, our excitement came to a screeching halt. The next morning, we did what we knew we had to: we backed out of the deal.

So there we were: more than four months, fifty-something apartments, seven bids, and this one near-hit later. We were still searching, still hoping, still empty handed. And I thought Manhattan could be tough.

A WALKING TOUR OF RED HOOK

With only one bus and no subways servicing all of Red Hook, this Brooklyn neighborhood remains off the grid—though guaranteed, that will change as more businesses, art studios, and, inevitably, fancy, new condos, move in. It's that exoticism and remoteness that make it especially fun to explore.

Although public transportation is limited, you can actually take a water taxi from Manhattan to Red Hook, enjoying harbor views en route and when you dock. Before heading up the main drag of Van Brunt, explore the studios, exhibitions, and performances at Pioneer Works, a massive multidisciplinary community center.

On to Van Brunt—it has a smattering of cool boutiques and plenty of good eating. Fort Defiance serves up Southern cooking and tiki cocktails, while the Good Fork infuses Korean ingredients into its comfort food menu. For something sweet, stop at Baked. From all the cookies, cupcakes, bars, and tarts, my favorite is the Brookster, a pie-shaped brownie with a chocolate chip cookie at its center.

Deviate from the main drag, and you'll find two Red Hook essentials: Steve's Authentic Key Lime Pies and Cacao Prieto. Steve's is a hole-in-the-wall establishment that abides by its own operating hours and focuses simply and sublimely on one thing: key lime pie made from all natural ingredients. Cacao Prieto is a small-batch rum distillery/chocolate factory that sources all its cacao from the owner's family farm in the Dominican Republic. The rum-filled bonbons are to die for, and the illustrated packaging of the chocolate tablettes make them the perfect gifts.

Then Comes Marriage

CHAPTER 6

Decadent Duck

It finally happened. After months of trying to figure out where I should steer my career or at least how to get out of that toxic job, I landed at another ad agency.

Not only was I relieved to be rid of Dennis's craziness and away from the cool kids' critical eyes, but I was actually excited about this new gig as well. The agency was new to town, an offshoot of a British firm and, as such, fresh with possibility. The growing staff hailed from all different countries and backgrounds—from France to Australia, editorial to entertainment, from just out of college to well into their fifties—making it an eclectic mix of personalities and talent. The work was challenging but familiar, and I was back in my element, slowly shedding those feelings of insecurity that had burrowed under my skin at the last job. It was good to feel connected and optimistic. It was good to be happy at work again.

I was equally as busy as I was happy, for Andrew and I had also—drumroll, please!—finally scored an apartment. Just before the market had slowed down for the summer, we had won a bidding war for a two bedroom with "great bones," to use some of the real estate lingo we picked up on the hunt. It had a good layout, good light, good closet space, and, the coup de grace, its very own washer and dryer. As far as we were concerned, we would be living in the lap of urban luxury. The second bedroom was spacious, giving us room to breathe once we lived together—and to grow, if all went according to plan.

But for all that our new apartment did have, it did not have a modern kitchen and bathroom. Once we closed, we got the co-op board's approval to undertake renovations. In addition to gutting the kitchen and bathroom, we decided to take my interior decorator father's advice and tear down a wall between the living room and dining room to create one giant common room, giving it a more modern feel. We were also installing built-in bookshelves, stripping, sanding, and staining the floors, and painting all the walls and ceilings. It had been eight marathon months from our first open house to now, and we were finally nearing the end of our real estate journey.

The renovations were introducing me to whole new side of Andrew. While I had forever bemoaned how laid-back he is, how all the date planning, communication instigating, and essential relationship bits fell to me, Andrew was all over these renovations. He was proudly donning a take-charge attitude, working with the contractors to get shit done. He'd often stop by our new apartment on his way to work to check on progress, directing the contractors on paint colors, shelf dimensions, appliance selection, and all the other details we were going to live with in our new home on a daily basis. He kept me updated, filling me in on what our tasks were for the weekend, where our budget stood, and what decisions still needed to be made. If I had ever thought he'd never initiate or be the proactive one in our partnership, I could now see I had been wrong. Apparently there had been a macho man hiding inside Andrew all this time, willing and able to take the lead, and I have to say, it was hot.

One morning as I was rushing down my East Village apartment building's seven flights of stairs to get to work, I noticed I could feel my boobs bouncing—a rare to virtually impossible sensation given my A cups. Not only did I realize they were bouncing, and therefore must have grown overnight, but they were sore. I stopped between floors three and four and felt myself up. Could it be? Was I pregnant?

A few weeks earlier, I had tried one of those ovulation kits the fertility specialist had recommended. At that point, I had been off the pill for six months and figured my system should have been free and clear to conceive if ever it would be. Once I saw the little smiley face signaling a surge in luteinizing hormone (LH), which indicated that I was ovulating, I called Andrew and told him to get to my place immediately. But could getting pregnant be as easy as a few days of overly enthusiastic sex?

I popped into the Duane Reade on my corner after work to get a pregnancy test, feeling totally conspicuous, as it was the first time I'd bought one since I was a teenager. I kept my eyes down as I paid, for some reason feeling as embarrassed as if I actually were a teen again. But any notion of being discreet was thrown out the window when the cashier gave me a big shout-out with my receipt: "Good luck!" he said with a toothy grin.

Back at my apartment, I closed the door to the bathroom even though Milo was the only one who might see me peeing on the test stick. I rested the stick flat on the counter per the instructions and went back out to the kitchen to pour myself some water. I rifled through the mail, and I checked my phone for messages. I changed into sweats and gazed out my bedroom window overlooking Third Avenue. It was clogged as always with taxis, buses, cyclists, and pedestrians. I had been perched in this spot in the East Village for nearly ten years, watching the neighborhood transform from modest walk-ups and grungy punks to glitzy condos and fancy college kids. Despite the dubious new reality, I was going to miss it when I was gone.

Long beyond the three minutes it took for a test result to appear, I made my way back to the bathroom for my moment of reckoning. It was positive.

I didn't shriek or laugh or cry with hysteric joy like they do in the commercials. Truthfully, I felt numb to any emotion. Although Andrew and I had talked about it, although we were hoping and planning for it, even though I did that ovulation test and we had sex for the sole purpose of getting pregnant, now that I was, I didn't know if I was ready for it. A new job, new apartment...new baby? What had I been thinking?

There are certain moments and scenes in those first couple of years with Andrew that still stick out in my mind. The next morning was one of them. We were meeting our contractor at the new apartment to check on how renovations were progressing. Inevitably, the estimated budget and time frame had been blown and every week we wondered anew: When would we finally get to move in? I hated not being able to control how long it was taking to complete everything. We had been living in limbo for months, waiting for so many things to come together and, with that little pregnancy test stick, there was now yet another factor to consider.

I rounded the corner to our new street, bright September sunlight beaming down through the trees. It was so unlike the deluge of honking taxis, double-parked trucks, halal carts frying up chicken, and chanting panhandlers back in Manhattan. A giant glass Richard Meier apartment tower stood guard on the corner, a major outlier among the early twentieth-century buildings that dominated the block. There were stray pedestrians heading off to work, walking their dogs, and pushing strollers, coffee and cell phones in hand. It was all so quaint and peaceful. I could see Andrew standing in front of our building awning, head piously bowed over his iPhone, the same way it was the very first time I saw him outside Park Bar.

This is it, I thought. *Everything changes as soon as I open my mouth.*

I quickened my pace to reach him and instead of saying anything, I handed him a baggie. Inside was the pregnancy stick, now displaying not one, but two little lines. Two lines that meant something was growing inside of me. Two lines that would dictate every decision we made from now on.

"Hi!" Andrew said with a smile, taking the baggie I was holding out, a quizzical look on his face. "What's this?"

I said nothing and instead watched his brow change from furrowed confusion to wide-eyed disbelief as he made out what the baggie contained.

"Oh my God, really?"

"Yup!"

"Oh. My. God." Andrew folded me into his arms.

"Can you believe it?!" I asked, burying my nose into his neck, still incredulous myself.

"No," he responded, sounding genuinely surprised. Andrew doesn't obsess about things the way I do. He had probably even forgotten about the ovulation test that sparked that particularly amorous three-day streak a while back. We pulled away and both laughed. Nervously, happily stunned. It didn't seem real. Aside from my tender breasts, which I was now very much aware of, I didn't feel what I had expected pregnancy would be like. No nausea or vertigo. No hormones making me eat copious amounts of pie and pickles or act loony and hyper-maternal. I had the same energy, was wearing the same clothes, and was going about my same business like any other Wednesday in September. Andrew and I stood indulging our how-in-the-world, oh-my-Lord, is-this-for-real stream-of-conscious thoughts before heading up to our apartment, which looked as though a bomb had gone off in it, sending us both to work with exploding thoughts and feelings.

Later in the day, I found some privacy to call the doctor I had seen earlier that year and she had me return to the fertility clinic for blood and urine tests. There, my pregnancy was officially confirmed. Because of my "advanced maternal age," the term given to women who seem to have prioritized work and independence a decade or two before getting pregnant,

I was to return to the clinic each week until I was three months along. Routine blood work would track the levels of my pregnancy hormones and an ultrasound would monitor fetal growth.

After my appointment confirming the news, everything was different—and yet the same. As major as this news was, it still belonged only to Andrew and me. In the meantime, the rest of the world still had its demands and expectations and wasn't slowing down. Besides, getting pregnant hadn't preoccupied us. It happened relatively quickly and easily. It had been an active choice yet a passive pursuit. Now that it had happened, *now that I was pregnant*, it mostly just felt surreal. It was weird having such a big secret and not being able to tell anyone about it because it was so early and uncertain. Anything could still happen. Anything—like being told there should be a heartbeat when there wasn't.

"Are you sure about the date?" asked the doctor during what was estimated to be my sixth week.

"Yeah, pretty sure," I said, thinking back and calculating when the ovulation kit had given us that smiley face to go forth and procreate.

"Well, we should be able to detect a heartbeat at this point," he said.

On each of my three visits, a different doctor had conducted the appointment, which made it somehow easier to believe that this one might not know what he was talking about.

He could be missing or overlooking something. "But we'll give it another week before we make any decisions," he said before wishing me a good day and leaving me to get dressed. His curt words weren't exactly a ringing endorsement, but the blood tests from that same morning acknowledged that my pregnancy hormones were still going up, which was an important sign. Maybe this guy was somehow misinformed about my status. Maybe the ovulation kit had been wrong and I had conceived after the window I was counting from. Or maybe karma was responding to my relative indifference to the news of being pregnant. In any case, I had to live with this secret—as uncertain as it was—for another week.

More eager than ever to move into our apartment, Andrew and I returned to it that Saturday to check again on how the renovations had progressed. I had been slowly packing up my apartment and pawning furniture, clothes, house-wares, and books. With each trip to a consignment store or charity drop-off, it felt like I was dismantling my life: my antique cast-iron bed from my grandfather's auction days that I'd slept in since the age of six. The giant *Restaurant de la Machine à Bougival* print by Maurice de Vlaminck I bought at the Musée d'Orsay as an exchange student in Paris and had hung framed in my bedroom ever since. The electric juicer and rice cooker, appliances that had made me feel so adult in my twenties and that I had toted from San Francisco to two apartments in New York and never used, not once. All these objects conjured different chapters of my life and varying levels of sentimentality. But the more boxes I packed, the less I allowed myself to be emotional about parting with anything. It was time to be doing this.

Unfortunately, when we got inside our apartment, it didn't look like we'd be living there anytime soon. There was debris—splintered wood and plaster from the wall that had been torn down, bits of metal, dismantled boxes—in different-sized heaps everywhere, covered in a layer of dust. Drop cloths were down in the living room and bedroom, but the paint was yet to go on the walls. The kitchen cupboards were installed, but the lack of counters and appliances still left gaping holes. Wires poked out of the walls. Bare bulbs dangled from ripped-out fixtures. The floors, which had long ago been stripped, sanded, and stained dark ebony, were covered with butcher paper that was torn and fraying along the edges but hopefully still protecting the new finish. Shouldn't the floors have been the last thing to get done, anyway?

Andrew put on a bright face to counteract my own crestfallen expression. "Why don't we go somewhere for brunch and then walk across the Brooklyn Bridge?" he asked. It was early October: cool, crisp, and sunny. I couldn't get the contractors to step it up. I couldn't get the doctor to offer certainty about my pregnancy's viability. And I sure didn't feel like facing another afternoon of schlepping pieces of my life to secondhand stores, so they could tell me how little it was all worth. But I could let Andrew call the shots. So we set out for eggs and pancakes and another Brooklyn ramble.

It didn't take long for certain things to start clicking. Andrew is not a big planner; he usually waits for my lead. But he had been very confident about the idea of walking across the Brooklyn Bridge—as if he had been thinking about it for more than the two seconds it seemed when he suggested it. And he was carrying his Jack Spade messenger bag, ordinarily reserved for work or picnic outings. If I really wanted to analyze things, he seemed inordinately smiley, but also just a little on edge.

We had shopped for engagement rings together several months earlier, and he knew I was starting to chafe at how long it was taking for the actual proposal to happen, especially now that I was maybe-maybe-not pregnant. So after our nondescript brunch at a Fort Greene restaurant with requisite reclaimed wood floors and Edison light fixtures, when we were about a quarter of the way over the bridge and Andrew ushered me out of the way of the bicyclists barreling past and the throngs of Italian and French tourists, my stomach began to lurch.

"Hi, babe." Andrew turned to me as if we hadn't been together since waking up hours earlier. He wore a big smile and just a little bit of a tremor.

"Hi." I grinned back at him, knowing this was it. He was about to propose. We were both filled with jitters and glee. We knew this moment was inevitable—we had been talking about getting married for the better part of the year—but it was still nerve racking. It was another huge step in a short period of time. He reached into his jacket pocket and took out a piece of paper and began telling me the story about why we were standing together where we were.

The Brooklyn Bridge was designed in the 1860s by John A. Roebling, a German immigrant and civil engineer from Pennsylvania. He was renowned for the suspension technology he used to build such bridges as the one over the Niagara Gorge at Niagara Falls and the Ohio River in Cincinnati. But after designing the Brooklyn Bridge using that same progressive technology, his involvement was short lived. As he was taking compass readings on a dock, his foot got crushed by a ferry. His toes were amputated, but within weeks, he died from tetanus. Before he passed away, Roebling placed his son Washington, also a civil engineer who had worked with his father on several other bridges, in charge of the project. But Washington, along with dozens of other workers, was soon also stricken with a debilitating illness: the bends, the result of surfacing too quickly from the compressed air chambers used to lay the bridge's underwater foundations. Washington escaped death but was inflicted with paralysis, deafness, and partial blindness. Determined to still be involved, he turned the responsibilities of the project's completion over to his wife, Emily, and watched the bridge's slow progression via telescope from their home in Brooklyn Heights.

Emily, Andrew emphasized, was no slouch. She had taken it upon herself to learn suspension technology and construction guidelines, while also tending to Washington's medical needs. She took over the daily chief engineer duties, relaying information from Washington to his assistants and reporting the progress of the bridge back to him. She developed an extensive knowledge of the strength of building materials, stress analysis, and cable construction. She dealt with politicians, engineers, construction workers, and everyone even tangentially associated with the project. She carried on with devotion for the *fourteen years* it took to complete the Brooklyn Bridge, the nation's first steel and cable suspension bridge. It spanned 1,600 feet from tower to tower—3,460 feet in total—and was built with as much love and devotion as engineering and ingenuity. And in the end, because of the combination of Washington's and Emily's perseverance as much as the elder Roebling's technology, it was a bridge that was six times stronger than it needed to be.

This was the kind of man I was going to marry. Andrew had chosen the Brooklyn Bridge to propose less for how beautiful and picturesque it is, or even for its symbolism in linking our two worlds of Manhattan and Brooklyn together, but for its auspicious origins in love and partnership. While we hadn't endured physical catastrophes or urban bureaucracy, we had weathered a few of our own modest tribulations and setbacks.

After Andrew pulled the ring out of his bag and we admired it on my finger, he opened a mini-bottle of champagne. It was more for ceremony than to drink as I was still holding on to the idea that I was pregnant, but still, we held our glasses of Veuve Clicquot and stared at the Manhattan skyline, staying in the moment for as long as possible. So much had happened since I had come home from Paris, so much remained still unknown—who knew what the future held next?

As we carried on with our walk after Andrew's beautiful proposal, he told me we were going out to celebrate that night and to wear something nice.

"Sweet! Where are we going?" I asked.

"I'm not telling."

"Have I been there before?"

"I don't think so."

"Have you?"

"No." I considered the possibilities. Il Cantinori and al di la, both dark and charming Italian restaurants, the first in Greenwich Village and the latter in Park Slope, were out, as we had celebrated anniversaries there. So too were Balthazar and Minetta Tavern, Keith McNally restaurants that we both loved for their buzzing brasserie atmospheres. It had to be elegant enough to get spiffed up for, but I didn't think Andrew would pick somewhere superextravagant. "What neighborhood?" I continued prodding.

"The Village."

"Is it the Waverly Inn?" I guessed after a moment.

"Nope."

"Two if by Land?" I asked, botching the name of One if by Land, Two if by Sea, the restaurant within a candlelit carriage house that is most notorious for its volume of marriage proposals.

"Nope," Andrew said. I thought to keep pressing, but instead I left it at that, delighted that I was going to be surprised with a special dinner reservation.

That night, donning a silk top and kitten heels, I was confused as Andrew and I walked near Washington Square Park in Greenwich Village. All I could think of was Babbo, but I knew Andrew had been there before. Il Mulino? Fedora? I was still trying to guess where we were going when he guided me down three steps of a townhouse and I saw the stately letters spelling it all out: Blue Hill.

Blue Hill was opened in the spring of 2000 by Chef Dan Barber; his brother, David; and sister-in-law, Laureen. At the time, they had modest expectations, humble self-regard, and the simple intention of opening a neighborhood bistro that would showcase Dan's talents. Sixteen years later, they—Dan in particular—have changed American dining.

Though Dan went to Tufts University and studied English and political science, he was interested in food and even started a supper club in his dorm room. After school, he leaned into his passion, going on to graduate from the French Culinary Institute. He spent a brief time baking bread at Nancy Silverton's acclaimed La Brea Bakery in Los Angeles, and then went to France, where he staged, or interned, for a year. These were logical progressions to opening his own restaurant, but "the original inspiration for Blue Hill actually came much earlier," Dan explains. "Growing up, David and I spent our summers with our grandmother on her farm in the Berkshires. She had this sense of responsibility about preserving the landscape, and that translated into my feelings about food, which is to some extent the responsibility attached to the way we eat or the place that we eat. The restaurant became a place to explore those ideas."

Asparagus season hit not long after Blue Hill first opened, and when Dan walked into the refrigerator that was filled to the gills with the chubby green spears after already cooking with it for days on end, he nearly lost it. Almost in a fit of rebellion, he decided that every dish served that night, from soup to ice cream, was going to have asparagus in it. It ended up being a seminal decision for the chef and the restaurant, as the critic Jonathan Gold was dining there that night. The review he later wrote lauded the restaurant and its devotion to seasonal ingredients, declaring it the epitome of farm-to-table dining. It was the start of Chef Barber becoming recognized as the most important voice in seasonable, sustainable farming and eating. "When we first opened Blue Hill, farm-to-table wasn't the established movement that it is today," he says. "In the last decade, diners have become a lot more curious—and a lot more demanding—about the food on their plates. People want to know where their food comes from and how it was grown. They're starting to engage with a new kind of recipe—the kind that begins, not in the kitchen, but in the fields and pastures."

Indeed, after their grandmother passed away and her farm fell into disrepair, the brothers strategically looked at how they could resurrect it. The answer was essentially bringing animals back: from dairy cows and goats to chickens and pigs, the symbiotic relationship between these free-ranging animals and the grass, grains, and land started producing rich, flavorful ingredients. This method is the gold star of farming practices. And at both restaurants—in 2004, the team opened Blue Hill at Stone Barns, a working farm and restaurant thirty miles north of the city that couldn't be a clearer example of what *farm-to-table* really means—the relationship the chef has with his farmers, the land, and ingredients comes through in every dish. "Chefs now have the opportunity to agitate change, creating trends that trickle down to almost every level of the food chain. So the question is, can chefs help us to see nature in a more enlightened way? Our role is always to pursue the best-tasting ingredients for our menus. What I've learned, though, is that if you are pursuing the best possible flavor, you are, by definition, also seeking the right kind of nutrition, the right kind of soil health. As chefs, we have the chance—and perhaps stronger still, the responsibility—to make those connections clear."

I felt so lucky to eat at this legendarily principled restaurant the night Andrew proposed. With our emotions sky high, yet also tinged with dark uncertainty, it was reassuring to be somewhere with a mission and message to the world—not to mention some of the city's best food. Blue Hill had just won the James Beard Outstanding Restaurant Award (in 2015, Blue Hill at Stone Barn would receive the same honor). It was also classically elegant and old-school New York: taupe banquettes, white tablecloths, and hushed tones. We were able to sink into comfort and decadence, enjoying our three-course dinner enveloped in our own private world within this greater one.

First up were these dainty heirloom vegetables, speared like lollipops on a "fence" of fine metal pricks. "I'm not a minimalist by nature," the chef explains of this simple yet exquisite dish, "but sometimes the stuff we get from the farm is so perfect, I feel like I shouldn't do much with it: just vegetables, naked, with salt and a little lemon vinaigrette." Andrew and I plucked the carrots, fennel, radishes, and greens one by one, relishing the powerful flavor contained within each, along with the snap, crunch, and wholesomeness. So simple and pure.

But it wasn't all so austere. We moved on to luscious potato gnocchi, fresh tilefish from Montauk, and my favorite, duck. Blue Hill gets its ducks from a local farm called Garden of Spices, where they're raised on grass, something that is rarely done in this country. "We cold smoke the legs for several hours—tenderizing the muscles from all that activity—and roast the breasts on the bone." The succulent meat, as decadent as it gets for me since I don't eat red meat, took me back to Paris, where I started really appreciating how sublime a piece of fowl could be. But that night, I was happily in New York, happily sated, firmly on the cusp of two worlds.

....

Although Andrew and I were both elated through the weekend as we shared our engagement news with family and friends, there was still a shadow hanging over us. All of this excitement was muddied with not knowing the status of my pregnancy. It felt almost dishonest to gush about our engagement and remain mum about the fact that either I was pregnant or had miscarried.

But the uncertainty wasn't long lived. When I went in for my next appointment, the doctor confirmed the fetus was no longer viable. Naturally we were upset, even though miscarriages are actually quite common, especially, as we had been warned, for someone my age. But the pregnancy was so early on—still "theoretical" in Andrew's words. I reached for the despair and sadness but instead got detachment. While I felt like I should have been more shaken up, the pregnancy hadn't affected our lives yet. We had so many things going on—finishing the apartment, moving in together, my new job, and now, our engagement—so much to be thankful for. We had our lives together before us. And though it seemed strange at the heels of loss, we were actually happy and encouraged by the fact that we *could* get pregnant. With this stew of contradictory emotions, Andrew and I did what was really our only option: we put on brave faces and cracked on.

DATE NIGHT!

Whether it's your first, fifth, or fiftieth, a great date brings you ever closer to your lover—and the city. It's that magical formula of romance and charm, food and drink, mystery and certainty. Like every couple who's been together at least a couple years, Andrew and I had some especially memorable date nights, along with our simple, everyday favorites.

Early on, our go-to spot was Terroir, an irreverent wine bar in the East Village (now in Tribeca). We'd rock out to the Stones, Beastie Boys, or whatever they were blaring and let the incongruously scruffy bartenders, who really know their stuff, guide us to some undiscovered Greek or Austrian vintage. Fun + boozy = sexy times.

My favorite movie theater in the city is the subterranean Angelika on Houston Street. Not only do they get the best movies, but you can also hear the rumbling of the subway underground, and it feels like it could be any year in New York City. Ditto for Arturo's, the coal-oven pizzeria just down the street. After seeing a great film—*Blue Jasmine* and *Before Midnight* come to mind—we'd walk over to Arturo's and complete the "timeless in New York" experience, listening to the *pizzeria's live jazz, drinking Chianti, and splitting a large pie. Nostalgic + cozy = happy place.*

Once we moved to Brooklyn, our date nights were less frequent but no less satisfying. Henry Public became a favorite. The charming Cobble Hill bar serves up an obscenely good turkey leg sandwich and masterful cocktails, and has a jazz trio that plays on Sunday afternoons. Rustic + humble = warm hearts.

CHAPTER 7

Hot Toddy to the Rescue

As the next couple of months unfolded, I was surprised by how much my independent self loved living with Andrew. All those months of pushing him away, fighting for space and to maintain my own life, I had worried that I might, I don't know, *freak out* once we moved in together. Thankfully for both of us, I didn't. Merging our furniture and belongings was as easy as pie. Our living styles and decor sensibilities totally meshed. We didn't battle for the bathroom or a certain side of the bed. Moving in together was the loveliest nonissue in the world.

So much so that I started thinking maybe I didn't want a baby after all. I'd look around our brand-new, uncluttered, elegantly decorated apartment, or think about the trips to Buenos Aires and Charleston we had taken that year, and realize a baby would put an end to all of that.

It would interrupt our newly formed, comfy routines and habits. It would destroy any notion of freedom and spontaneity. And forget about keeping our first joint furniture purchase, a gorgeous gray velvet couch, stain free. A baby would mean no more romantic weekend getaways. No more buzzy nights out over fish bowl–sized manhattans. No more weekends that magically unfolded hour by hour as we trekked from bar to restaurant to park to another bar to another restaurant, until we wound up back home having great sex. Would I be okay with a life without these luxuries? Was I ready for a whole new reality and world of responsibility?

Contemplating these questions brought up some deeper-seated ones. What did it mean that I had never pursued getting pregnant in my twenties and thirties? Was I even supposed to be a mom? Did I want to be one? Maybe I wouldn't be good at it. Maybe I'd have a kid and then lament the decision, making all of our lives miserable. Maybe I was just too selfish. I'd been living a carefree life for decades now. Aside from career obligations, I didn't have to make many concessions or compromises for anyone. I wondered if I would ever be happier than I was right there and then: in a new job, a happy relationship, baby free.

I didn't say any of this out loud; I didn't feel like I could— not even to Andrew. The subject of parenthood had been broached, actions had been taken, and the journey was underway. But after the miscarriage, I was more than a little ambivalent about trying to get pregnant again.

I found it easy enough not to dwell on it for too long. I knew my body needed time to recover. And I frankly doubted that my system was capable of successfully conceiving. I figured the miscarriage had been a signal that I was too old to have a baby, that I had pushed my luck, waited too long, and that if I tried again, I'd have the same fate waiting. So rather than think about how potentially reckless I'd been in thinking I could have a baby in my forties, I put it out of my mind and focused on Andrew and the falling-in-love phase I was re-experiencing now that we lived together.

On weekends, we took long urban strolls, crisscrossing Brooklyn on a more organic level, discovering the cool neighborhood spots that weren't touted on local blogs or magazines and had nothing to do with real estate recon. We went to Speedy Romeo, an Italian restaurant that has a pizza topped with Provel, a processed cheese popular in the Midwest that was virtually unknown in the Northeast. A Bed–Stuy B&B that hosts jazz concerts followed by fish fries in its town house parlor on weekend nights. And Cacao Prieto, a rum distillery that doubles as a beans-to-bar factory, producer of killer single origin 72 percent dark chocolate bars and rum-filled truffles.

Or we'd just stay home all weekend, trying new recipes from *Bon Appetit* and settling in for a marathon session of

Girls, House of Cards, True Detective, or whatever our latest obsession was. Life was comfortable. With Andrew, I learned that "doing nothing" was awfully fun. I intentionally dialed back my freelance, a colossal shift after building it up for so many years, but I now felt more protective of my time, inclined to spend it with Andrew rather than keeping up with and writing about the city's evolving restaurant scene. My book launch was also now well behind me. After birthing that enormous project, then dealing with the frenetic apartment hunt and still feeling depleted from that toxic job, it was a relief to let some of my ambition slide. My old life across the river felt years in the distance, and I was okay with it. After all, who needs flashy nights out and trendy new restaurants when you have Netflix and the man you love?

After all my worrying about moving in with Andrew, who would have guessed that my existential crisis would be about living in Brooklyn?

This move was exactly what I had wanted. For years, I had dreamed about it, planned for it, fought for it—and apparently had done it all wearing rose-tinted glasses. I had been naive and idealistic in my fantasizing of the borough and the life I'd have there. I didn't realize that in moving forward, I'd be leaving certain things behind.

First, there was the pain of missing Manhattan itself. It was the city that had been my home for over a decade, so dazzling and filled with excitement and promise that it had lured me back from Paris. It was my love and muse, representing energy and possibility, stimulation and desire. It was a safe harbor in a world that seemed to value freethinking and diversity less and less. It was also magnificently, overwhelmingly, ridiculously dirty; maddening; and irrational, which was often its very thrill. That and the constant rotation of new bars, restaurants, bakeries, boutiques, exhibitions, and performances that you could never keep up with. Manhattan's intensity is nonstop—the wailing taxi horns, swerving buses, aggressive pedestrians, and the general neuroses, attitudes, and craziness that emanate from all the people that occupy every last square foot of space. As much as it can wear you down, it's addictive. It's a reminder of what it is to feel alive. Like a physical presence, when you're not near it, you crave it. And now that I didn't wake up in Manhattan's thrum every morning, I felt like I had gone through a divorce, like I had been cleaved from my former life.

It wasn't only the physical move from Manhattan, but also what the move to Brooklyn represented. When I packed up my 550-square-foot apartment in the East Village and toted all my belongings to consignment shops and, in the end, the curb, I was saying good-bye to ten years of my life—my "swinging" thirties, no less. It had been an era of being single and carefree, hitting the town with AJ, carousing in packs of partygoers, having no obligation except to have a good time and make it to work the next day. All those epic moments and memories of randomly falling into conversations with strangers and winding up going to parties in penthouse apartments with them until 3:00 a.m. were now history. Despite wanting this new life in Brooklyn and intentionally steering myself toward it, despite all the anticipation, it felt shocking.

Then there was the disappointment with Brooklyn itself. It felt sacrilegious to even *think* it, what with all the fawning the borough now got in newspapers and magazines, both locally and abroad, not to mention all those other former Manhattanites who now lived in Brooklyn and insisted it was the only place where cool things were happening, but it was true: I was disappointed. Brooklyn had become mythical in my mind—this amazing place where I envisioned a fabulously bohemian lifestyle, sipping rosé at outdoor cafés, and brushing elbows with the literary set. I thought I'd be going to underground dinner parties, meeting editors and doughnut makers, surfing waves of the next artisanal food trends, and listening to an indie synth pop soundtrack throughout it all. I thought I'd feel as cool living in Brooklyn as everyone, including me, had made the borough out to be.

But instead of walking to work as I had in Manhattan, I now had to fight my way onto a jam-packed subway twice a day. Instead of being a stone's throw away from Trader Joe's,

Whole Foods, and the biggest, best farmers' market in all of New York, I had a measly bodega on my corner. Instead of a charmed, cultural utopia, Brooklyn felt like the burbs. I felt middle-aged and alienated. Irrelevant and defeated. I knew I couldn't stay out dancing all night with AJ forever, and truthfully, I no longer wanted that life. But the emotional part of my brain still had to catch up with the rational part.

Speaking of rational, wedding planning was anything but.

"What about a restaurant?" Andrew posed. Two months after getting engaged, we were trying to figure out where and when we were going to get married. But thinking and talking about ideas so far hadn't gotten us closer to any sort of promising plan. Unlike the apartment search, we didn't have a clear idea of how to get what we wanted. Poking around the requisite wedding websites and magazines, not knowing really where to begin, I felt in over my head. Bridesmaids? Bouquets? A billowing ball gown and tiara? What was the point of it all? Send me to a country where I didn't speak the language or drop me in the middle of a different culture anytime, but this? This was foreign territory.

I was now forty-one—twelve years older than the average American bride. As much as I love going to weddings—tearing up during the vows, dive-bombing the cheese platter during cocktail hour, pogo dancing to Kris Kross with utter abandon—I didn't take mental notes for when my day arrived. I never knew if such a day *would* arrive. But if and when it did, I knew it wouldn't be your typical country-club setup. Despite watching umpteen hours of *Say Yes to the Dress* on TLC with my mom over the years, I myself wasn't looking to find "the dress." I found the show's eye-rolling personalities entertaining, but it made me queasy every time I saw how vicious family members could be with their sartorial opinions, or how much pressure mothers and sisters and best friends put on each other. I didn't want to look at invitations and party favors, create a Pinterest board of inspiration, or decide on thematically appropriate centerpieces. I was excited to marry Andrew, but I just couldn't get excited about all this other stuff.

Andrew and I shared a pretty simple vision for our wedding: we wanted it to be relatively intimate, have a sense of place, and be something that would not clear out what remained of our savings account. In our minds, this was a modest ask. We weren't envisioning big bands, big limos, or big hoopla. We weren't asking for anything to be "the ultimate" and had no delusions of having a "dream" wedding. Perfection wasn't even part of the plan. We thought we should be able to throw a party for our families and friends without going into debt. Ha.

That first book I had proposed when I moved to New York at the turn of the millennium? It was a nontraditional wedding guide. I had done tons of research on the wedding industry back then and saw that as soon as the word *engaged* passed your lips—*cha-ching*—prices notched up stratospherically. I knew Andrew and I were in for it. I just didn't realize how much. Somehow, my brain had skipped over the fifteen intervening years, since I had done so much research and was still thinking in terms of 2001 costs. Once we started talking to facility managers and getting estimates, we were blown away.

We focused our initial research and planning on Brooklyn. Despite my qualms about living there, it was our home together. It was part of our story. And, I still had to admit, it was charming. We loved the idea of bringing our families and friends here to see its rough-at-the-edges beauty and also figured it would cost less than Manhattan, the most expensive place in the country to host a wedding. And yet it was beyond our reach. At the venues we visited, everything was adding up to tens of thousands of dollars, was booked over a year in advance, or was just not our style.

So, yes, in theory, a restaurant seemed like a great idea. The previous summer, Ben and Merrill had gotten married at one in South Slope called Lot 2. We had loved its intimacy, uniqueness, and delicious family-style platters of roasted chicken and chocolate cake. But restaurants posed a whole different set of logistical and financial challenges. "Unless we're going to pony up what they can clear in a night, we'll have to do a daytime wedding," I thought aloud to Andrew. "Besides, Merrill was friends with the owners, and we're not friends with any bar or restaurant owners." I paused. "Are we?" I asked thinking maybe, miraculously, I was forgetting about some crucial relationship one of us had with a chef or restaurateur who had a place that could accommodate one hundred people on a Saturday night and would be willing to do so at cost. But then I realized, nope, I wasn't.

"How important do you think food is?" Andrew asked, shifting gears. We had discovered a private club near our apartment. It had two floors of old-school charm—carved mahogany walls, giant fireplaces, stained-glass windows—and it couldn't have been more convenient or compelling. We kept trying to convince ourselves it was the right choice. It was a little run down, but it was priced well enough that we could invite everyone we wanted, plus their kids—which was another decision we were struggling with, especially since we both had older brothers with kids, and we wanted our own nieces and nephews there. But this place had truly sad food. We had been invited to dine there to help seal the deal, but after a salad drowning in sugary dressing, limp rings of fried calamari, and pasta and fish as uninspired as my college cafeteria's, our hopes for having found our place were dashed.

I looked at Andrew. "We can't have crappy food. We just can't."

"I know," he sighed and leaned away from the dining room table that occupied half of our great room. We were both gazing at the Charlie Brown Christmas tree we had on

HOT TODDY TO THE RESCUE

the other side of the room: small and misshapen, it managed to be endearing with our motley ornaments hanging from it. All along, we had been talking about a summer wedding, but given how things were going, six months didn't seem like enough time to pull it off.

"Connecticut?" Andrew scrunched up his brow, so unwilling to be defeated that he was returning to earlier ideas we had explored. It turns out that I do have a traditional side and found the idea of getting married where I grew up pretty cool, so we had blasted through three venues near my hometown one recent weekend. It was fun to envision a fabulous celebration on a sprawling green lawn along the water, where all my friends' and cousins' kids would run around chasing fireflies while the adults got tipsy on gin cocktails. But those fantasies were also squashed once we learned we'd have to rent tents, tables, chairs, dishes, tablecloths, lighting, Porta-Potties, and valet drivers for our bucolic outdoor vision in addition to paying a venue fee. Connecticut would be just as expensive as any city venue we had seen.

In fact, wedding planning was starting to have a frightening resemblance to our apartment hunt. Andrew and I started devoting all our free time to the search, developing strategies and second-guessing our choices. We felt like we were in fierce competition with other couples, duking it out for first dibs on spaces we looked at, all while trying to keep calm and carry on. Money became a weirdly distorted concept, as if paying $200 for one person's dinner and multiplying that by 100 was totally reasonable, or spending $6,000 on floral arrangements that would die sad, lonely deaths after their five hours in the spotlight could be justified.

We struggled with how to balance our guest list and finances: to invite everyone we wanted, we'd have to torpedo our budget. But keeping it small meant we couldn't accommodate children or even all of our friends. Since every venue was dependent on both capacity and budget, we went in circles, changing our minds and direction on a weekly basis. Nothing felt exactly right. And while we didn't have delusions that the wedding would be perfect, we sure as hell wanted to feel good about it. We were going to drop tens of thousands of dollars on what was essentially a five-hour party and humbly thought we shouldn't have to settle.

There were plenty of times we were tempted to just throw in the towel and not throw a wedding. Plenty of times a hot toddy was needed to cool off. "Let's keep thinking," I said, as Andrew rose from the table, putting his warm hands on my shoulders. "Something will pop up. How about a drink?"

Overheard at Sharlene's:
"She has a rock collection."
"Facebook is for losers."

"Want to hear my mushroom story?"

Every neighborhood should be so lucky to have a bar like Sharlene's. Located on Flatbush Avenue, the same traffic-clogged street that we had nearly lived on, it's been a no-frills, no-attitude neighborhood staple since 2009, though it feels like it's been untouched for generations.

Sharlene's is so innocuous, it could be anywhere in the country: Milwaukee, Wisconsin; Fort Smith, Arkansas; Ramsey, New Jersey—we've all been to Sharlene's. The bar is wood, and the floor is linoleum. The lighting is not too dark, not too bright, often glowing with strings of seasonal bulbs. There's a token jukebox and pinball machine. The music runs from Motown dance tracks to angry nineties metal. Because it could be anywhere, it has universal appeal. Pop in on a week night and find an old-timer in khakis and a Hawaiian shirt, reading the paper and drinking a Red Stripe, a solo girl with Princess Leia braids sipping a gin and tonic, and a couple of big-bellied dudes in baseball caps, catching up over pints.

What I immediately loved about it was that it wasn't trying to be anything it's not. I was still struggling to feel at home in Brooklyn, with its rash of twee restaurants and bars and dearth of normal, quality places to eat or drink. At Sharlene's, there is no small-batch anything. No bespoke cocktail list. No visiting mixologists or bartenders in suspenders with groomed facial hair. And not a lick of reclaimed wood or taxidermy in sight. It's no wonder, coming from Sharlene Frank.

Having grown up in Windsor Terrace and Sheepshead Bay, Sharlene is a product of old school Brooklyn. She had been tending bar at Commonwealth in Park Slope when Mooney's Pub, a popular Irish bar on Flatbush that had been around since 1986, closed. After years of bartending, she was ready to take the next step. She cashed in her savings, approached two former bosses to come aboard as business partners, and signed a lease to take over the space. And so, Sharlene's was born.

We discovered it to be the perfect sanctuary that winter. A five-minute walk from our apartment, the dark and cozy, down-to-earth, friendly, and forgiving vibe of the bar gave us a place to take a break from wedding stress and strategizing. And an excuse to drink hot toddies.

Naturally, the toddies are nothing fancy at Sharlene's. True to the original formula, it's a squeeze of a few lemon wedges into the bottom of a glass mug, a drizzle of some honey, a pour of bourbon, some boiling water from the hot pot, and then a few cloves are tossed in for flavor.

Andrew and I sat at the end of the long wooden bar, watching the bartender make our drinks, taking in the room's quiet chatter. Within two minutes, he slid them before us and gave us a nod before moving along. Comfort was served.

"Cheers, babe," Andrew said, lifting his mug to mine.

"Cheers," I returned. "To something popping up."

"To something popping up soon."

I took a sip of the slightly tart, slightly sweet, bracingly strong hot drink, knowing there was indeed a formula out there for a wedding that we'd love.

. . . .

In hindsight, wedding planning wasn't that bad. After the initial shock of prices and tail chasing on location and venues, things came together rather quickly.

Realizing we had to expand our search—again, just as we had in our apartment hunt—we were surprised to ultimately find an affordable venue that we loved in Manhattan: the New Museum on the Bowery, a once-derelict strip that now hops with acclaimed restaurants, karaoke bars, and underground clubs. One of the two caterers the museum partnered with auspiciously hailed from City Bakery, one of my favorite eateries in the city. Once we had those big decisions of venue and food made, it was easy enough to cull a list of vendors and start securing the remaining details.

We were so relieved to have some clarity and move forward and were just about to sign a contract for an August wedding when Milo, in his typical overly affectionate manner, head-butted me in the chest one morning as I loafed in bed. I gasped out loud from the pain—and then once more from the realization of what that pain meant: I was pregnant again.

CHEERS TO THE GOOD OLE BARS

As much as I love a fancy cocktail bar or the occasional hipster hangout, sometimes you just want...a bar. No fuss, no crowds, no drinks with more than three ingredients—just a place for a pint or G&T and a good conversation.

Cavernous and innocuous, Tom & Jerry's is on the border of Manhattan's Nolita, NoHo, and SoHo neighborhoods, making it the ideal meeting place. There's sometimes a movie playing the back or a game on the TV, and there's always space to hang out.

As spacious as Tom & Jerry's is, Park Bar is small. Just off Union Square, it's clean, considered, and absolutely nothing out of the ordinary—the perfect place for a quick rendezvous (or to meet your future husband).

The Half King in Chelsea isn't just a bar; it's more of a pub, also a restaurant, has outdoor space, regular literary readings and photo exhibits, and is co-owned by journalist Sebastian Junger. But for all that it is, it's not overwrought or pretentious, which makes it a good ole bar by my standards.

Thanks to its candle lighting and narrow, intimate rooms, Von is a great spot for dates. Thanks to deep offering of beers, wines, and cocktails, and its location just off of Bowery, it's also great for nearly any occasion.

CHAPTER 8

Make Mine a Double (Scoop)

Back to the fertility clinic I went. This time around, my weekly check-ins were more fraught, as I kept waiting for something to go wrong. I'd hold my breath as soon as the wand of the ultrasound machine was in the doctor's hand, not wanting anything to prevent me from hearing what I was hoping for: the sound of a little heart, beating upwards of 150 times a minute. And week after week, I heard it. It was detected at six weeks—the point which the earlier doctor had failed to hear it—and continued to beat strongly every week thereafter. My pregnancy hormones continued to rise. Soon, I cleared the critical twelve-week mark of when most miscarriages occur. I was then in the second trimester and could breathe easier—at least in theory. "It's still early" became my tentative refrain as I shared the news with family and friends. The caution was for me as much as anyone else; thanks to my "advanced maternal age" and earlier miscarriage, I didn't feel like I could fully trust things would work out. But once several genetic tests, including Down syndrome, came back negative and I discovered it was a girl—a *girl*!—who seemed to be growing, breathing, and developing normally, I started believing that everything was okay. As my girlfriend Elisa said, "This is your baby."

With the radical changes coming our way, Andrew and I decided to bump up our wedding. I was due in October. August 23, the date we had nearly secured at the museum, would be pushing it. Who knew how I would be feeling at seven months—swollen, cranky, on bed rest?—never mind what kind of dress would fit my as of yet unformed baby bump. As luck would have it, the museum was still free two Saturdays in June, so we jumped on one of them, starting to plan for a wedding that was now just a few months away.

So there I was: forty-one years old, taking prenatal vitamins, and obsessing about what I was going to wear on my wedding day. After all the years of dating and gallivanting, career tracking and traveling abroad, attending friends' weddings and baby showers, and never knowing if and when it was going to be my turn, I was pregnant and engaged to be married. It was crazy enough to make me laugh out loud—or maybe that was the hormones.

Any ambivalence I had once felt about getting pregnant

metamorphosed into joy. Maybe my earlier doubts had simply been a defense mechanism. Maybe all these new hormones surging around my body flipped a switch inside me to ensure that I felt like an elated mom-to-be. Or maybe it was exactly what Elisa had said. *This* was my baby. This pregnancy was for keeps, and it was exactly the way things were supposed to work out.

I let myself revel in these new feelings, modestly blushing when friends and colleagues euphorically responded to the news. "Omigod, you're pregnant?! Congratulations!" they said with big hugs and electric smiles. It never ceased to amaze me how generous people were with their happiness and affection, even those whom I barely knew. It made me feel special but, at the same time, gave me pause for thought. It was like getting pregnant and becoming a mom was life's crowning achievement. Didn't they know that I had published a book? Had become a rare female creative director in advertising? Had found a good man in New York City? Talk about achieving the impossible. But even I, who proudly beat my chest about following my own path through life, had to admit it was fun having people cluck over me during this traditional period.

I was also filled with giddy disbelief when I caught my profile in a mirror. Me, *pregnant*! I loved watching my belly slowly inflate like a balloon. There was a joyful freedom to no longer having control over my body and what shape it was taking. I knew I was going to get bigger and bigger, and no one could say one word or raise an eyebrow—it is an invaluable carte blanche issued to pregnant women. Considering the typical scrutiny our bodies get on an everyday basis, I gladly accepted the free pass.

There was a little person growing inside of me, and she was going to do what she was going to do. All I had to do was make the best decisions to keep her safe and healthy. I paid attention to what I ate but for wholly new reasons. Eschewing the Twizzlers and gummies at the office for the first time in my life had nothing to do with how many calories I had already had at lunch or how tight my jeans felt. It was all about regarding this little person's needs. Knowing corn syrup has absolutely no nutritional value hadn't been enough to stop myself from binging on sticky-sweet garbage for four decades, but I certainly couldn't justify ingesting such crap when it went directly to her. I've always been mindful of what I eat (well, it's all relative) and grateful for my healthy body, but this was a whole new level of appreciation. I found it amazing what a woman's body, *my* body, was capable of doing. And finally, I had boobs.

But I saw the other side too. Months of weekly visits to the fertility clinic had opened my eyes, sparking new compassion for the entire female species. The clinic buzzed in the wee morning hours with hopeful patients of every age, size, color, and sexuality trying to get pregnant. I may have been ambivalent about having a child for years, but witnessing all these women in different stages of desperation and hope, fear and determination made me realize how thin the line is between indifference and insensitivity. We are surrounded by so many women without knowing who are going through the pain of miscarrying or not being able to conceive. So many women who want to become mothers but who don't have partners or stability or healthy eggs and feel the pressure of time running out. Women who graciously smile upon hearing your news or seeing your belly but who are crying inside. There are so many complicated situations and imperfect choices, and until you face your own obstacles, it's just assumed that you can, and will, get pregnant.

It wasn't just the strangers at the clinic. I had married friends attempting IVF, both successfully and unsuccessfully. Single friends vacillated between feeling grateful for their independence and worrying about if they'd ever meet anyone and whether they should freeze their eggs—feelings I had experienced firsthand. Some of their perspectives were calm and matter of fact: "If it happens, it happens." Others expressed their deep angst and pain during raw, vulnerable moments. I understood it all, and there were moments when I felt guilty about how relatively easy I had it. It's one thing to not know if you want to have children, another being told that you can't. Now that I was pregnant, I felt beyond lucky for my good fortune. I understood nothing is guaranteed.

After the twelve-week mark in my pregnancy, I had switched from weekly check-ins at the fertility clinic to less frequent appointments with an obstetrician. The waiting room at her practice was calmer and emptier, despite there being actual babies everywhere. I also noticed all the new moms and pregnant women seemed about my age—it all seemed very Brooklyn. When I brought up these observations to my OB, she confirmed that there is indeed an uptick of older women having kids, which can make her job tricky. Women in their thirties get sensitive when she brings up their age and fertility, she said; they don't want a reminder or pressure about their biological clocks. Yet as a doctor, she has to be clear about the risks of waiting. She has more and more clients in their late thirties and early forties for whom getting pregnant is a challenge or rife with complications, and then they desperately wish they had done something about it when they were younger—the independent woman's catch-22.

And at the other end of the spectrum, my OB shared all these crazy success stories: The forty-eight-year-old, pregnant with IVF twins. Women who conceive naturally at forty-five after multiple rounds of failed IVF. And then there are the growing number of patients like me: technically single and pregnant, having rolled the fertility dice before committing to a man and marriage.

I know it's a cliché, but ice cream was one of my top pregnancy indulgences. Whereas splitting a pint used to be an occasional weekend activity for me and Andrew, we were suddenly killing one on a near-daily occurrence. It didn't help that the days were getting longer and warmer, and the best ice cream shop in all of Brooklyn, Ample Hills, was within dangerous proximity of our apartment.

Ample Hills was started by a husband-and-wife team: Brian Smith and Jackie Cuscuna. At the age of forty, Brian was a screenwriter of "bad monster movies" for the SyFy channel. He and Jackie, a high school teacher, had a four-year-old and a one-year-old. Every summer, they vacationed with family in the Adirondacks in upstate New York. Throughout it all, Brian was slightly obsessed with ice cream. "It always sat in the back of my head," he says of his lifelong relationship with the frozen dessert. Which is partly why he looked forward to these summer vacations: they were filled not only with quality family time and relaxation, but they also added motivation to dig deeper into his passion. "We had ice cream socials," Brian remembers of the summer trips. "We'd make ice cream for dozens of people, very idyllically cranking on a hand-crank ice cream machine, testing out flavors on people." Brian was knowingly, not knowingly, planting the seeds for a midlife career change.

After a few of these summers, the couple agreed that opening an ice cream shop was viable. With his career not exactly stalling but also not taking him to Steven Spielberg levels of success, Brian felt it was time. The itch wasn't going away. All kinds of wild and wacky flavors begged to be made. He'd been taking his son on expeditions around New Jersey, Staten Island, and other surrounding towns, checking out ice cream parlors: the ambiance and styles, the flavors and menus, all the while trying to figure out what they could do different. Once he and Jackie felt they had a business plan, the space, along with the critical mass, they decided to go for it.

Brian's recon helped inform several things he knew were critical to making his vision a success. Almost as much as creating ice cream, he wanted to foster a sense of community. He wanted his brand to be old-timey in execution. And he wanted all the ingredients of the ice cream, from peppermint patties to pistachio brittle, to be homemade. "From the beginning, I knew I wanted to make everything from scratch, and to do it in front of everyone, so they'd be invited into the narrative," Brian says, clearly influenced by his initial career as a storyteller. And, true Brooklynites, Brian and Jackie insisted on dairy cows that are grass fed and hormone free.

Ample Hills opened in May of 2011 with twenty-four flavors. Within four days, they'd sold out of their entire inventory, shutting the scoop shop down for a week. "It's a good story in hindsight," Brian says, "but at the time, it was terribly stressful." By the time Andrew and I lived in the neighborhood, a year and a half after Ample Hills' dramatic debut, they had found their footing. They adeptly balanced supply and demand, and when they did periodically sell out of a flavor, it was just because it was new and *that* delicious.

"The goal of flavor creation is to reach the seven-year-old inside the forty-seven-year-old," Brian explains of their instant connection with customers. While other ice cream start-ups in the city—and there have been plenty launches since Ample Hills, including OddFellows (2013), Morgenstern's (2014), and Ice & Vice (2015), to name a few—have found their success in offbeat flavors like avocado, extra virgin olive oil, red bean, and chorizo caramel, they aren't made in the same spirit of evoking the fun and play of childhood that Brian finds essential. It's a different brand of creativity.

Even though it inevitably meant waiting in a long line, I loved being the one to go to Ample Hills to pick up a pint because it also meant sampling the flavors. Each one is sweet and creamy, über-rich, and totally original. They're loaded with so many ingredients you never tire of taste testing them. There's ooey gooey butter cake, a full-flavor vanilla that's studded with chunks of rich, dense Saint Louis–style cake; the munchies, a salty-sweet pretzel-infused ice cream chock-full of Ritz crackers, potato chips, M&M's, and more pretzels; Nonna D's oatmeal lace is brown-sugar-and-cinnamon ice cream chunked with homemade oatmeal cookies; and their signature flavor, salted crack caramel, which involves caramelizing large amounts of sugar on the stovetop until it's nearly burnt, giving it a bitterness that distinguishes their version from all the other salted caramels out there.

When I was pregnant, it was easy to rationalize bringing home two pints instead of one, since it was always so hard to decide exactly which flavor to get. And then it just seemed efficient to buy three at a clip—ostensibly the three would last for the week, though they never did. As we compulsively pounded the decadent dessert night after night, I hid behind my baby bump, where I happily couldn't detect those hundreds of extra, creamy calories, wherever they might be landing, and hoped I wouldn't have to do major damage control after giving birth.

Meanwhile, as my belly ballooned, Ample Hills' success skyrocketed. Brian and Jackie opened a second location that summer in Gowanus—not far from Four & Twenty Blackbirds. They were touted on the Food Network and as one of Oprah's "Favorite Things." The following year, they published their own cookbook, and within five years of opening their first scoop shop, Ample Hills had expanded to six locations between Brooklyn and Manhattan and had a seventh shop, operated by Disney, on Disney's BoardWalk in Florida. They started distributing their pints in supermarkets and later secured funding to build a giant factory in Red Hook to sustain a constantly expanding distribution plan.

You wouldn't know it by their rapid ascension to ice cream dominance, but caution has guided their way. "The goal is to build out an anti-chain chain," Brian explains, fully aware that the charm of Ample Hills is that it's small, independently owned, and has quirks that locals appreciate. Every time they add a new scoop shop, they're mindful of creating at least one flavor that's unique to that location, like It Came Out of Gowanus, "the deepest, darkest, murkiest chocolate ice cream," in Brian's words, that's chock-full of white chocolate pearls, a nod to the waterway's once-prolific bivalves; chocolatey "crack cookies" made with hazelnut paste; and Grand Marnier–laced brownies. To foster community, they always include an experiential aspect—a playroom for kids, a party room, commissioned artwork—that is "not cookie-cutter." Jackie has designed all the custom tables, which are collages of vintage ads and ice cream photos, mixed with contemporary photos of their own family and fans from the different neighborhoods, each one unique. "It's terrifying because we're growing pretty quickly. The fear is that we'll implode from the pressures of it and destroy the very authenticity of what created it to begin with."

But the couple has managed to not only maintain Ample Hills' authenticity while growing to national recognition, but has also done it all while raising their two kids, now ten and seven. In the early days, Jackie was still teaching and she'd come to the original location in Prospect Heights after school, to run the front of the house and deal with staffing and resourcing. Later on, Brian would go pick the kids up from school and bring them to the shop, where they would do homework at the counter, and he developed ice cream flavors and products in the kitchen. When Jackie finally left her job at the school and joined Ample Hills full-time in 2015, she created internships for her old students to be "Amployees" at their scoop shops. In every way possible, Brian and Jackie have remained committed to running the business as a true family and community affair, and it's an investment that has paid off.

The other side of commitment is having the strength to each be alone—which has always been one of the things I love about Andrew. Once we were on firm ground, confident in where we stood with each other, he never begrudged my occasional desire for a solo outing, be it an afternoon to myself, a weekend with girlfriends...or a trip to Paris.

That spring, somewhere between clearing all the genetic tests and throwing a wedding, I flew to Paris for a week. It was something that we had talked about doing together, but Andrew had a restrictive vacation allotment and, truthfully, not as much of a burn to go. He decided he should save his vacation time for our honeymoon, but he encouraged me to go.

So I went. I ate. I Vélib'd. I got to share my news about

being pregnant in person with friends who always knew me as a proud single girl. When I told Mel, she laughed loudly and threw her arms around me. "When is she due?" she asked with her witchy sixth sense, not having been told yet that it was a girl. She had always had faith that I'd meet someone and get pregnant, and it was so gratifying to see her genuine delight.

These were the moments that filled my soul. It reminded me of how much happiness I had found in Paris. But I had also had seriously low moments when I wondered what I was doing with my life—if I were destined to be alone, and if becoming a mother would ever be an option to me. It seemed almost surreal that I was now back with these questions happily answered.

Yet visiting was also bittersweet. Being there made me realize that Paris was firmly in the past. Yes, my past, my story, but the city didn't belong to me the same way it used to. When I'd first visited Paris after moving home to New York, it was always a great feeling of reunification. I saw friends and acquaintances, went back to favorite places, and felt wonderful and comfortable, things not having changed that much. I knew Paris was part of me and that even though I had chosen to leave it, I still had a rightful place there; a couple of years as a resident had given me an insider's access and status.

But it had now been two years since that rocky trip with Andrew, four years since I had lived there. So much had changed, and I felt my place and voice in Paris was but a blip, replaced by a new generation of expats who blogged and tweeted about it. They had inroads and friends, and were part of the fabric and scene that had evolved so much that it was foreign to me. I realized I no longer had that intimate familiarity; I didn't have credibility or connections the way I used to.

It was a bit sad but mostly liberating. More than anything, being in Paris alone, pregnant, knowing it was likely my last time to be there solo was a gift. I had wanted to reconnect with "my" city, to indulge in old behaviors, relive memories, and spend quality time there. And I did, and loved every minute of it.

But I was excited to go back home. To return to Brooklyn. To Andrew. To my future chapter.

Back from Paris, it was back to reality. I was a pregnant woman and it was time to go for a level two scan, when they do an intensive ultrasound to make sure the fetus's skeleton, body parts, and internal organs are developing as they should be.

Andrew hadn't yet accompanied me to a doctor's appointment, which so far had been pretty quick and rote. But this one warranted his presence. After all, it's a whole different ball game when you hear a teeny heart beating at warp speed or see that alien-like object floating around the screen in front of you. I felt like a pro by now, hopping up on the table, leaning back into the crinkly paper, and folding my top up and pants down, so the technician could smear my belly with the gel that helped guide the ultrasound's wand.

In the darkened room, she quietly explained everything she was looking at on the screen. "There's the left chamber, and there's the right—that's the heart," the technician said, pointing out this itty-bitty pulsating bit on the screen. Andrew and I looked at each other in disbelief, like we did for nearly an hour, as the technician zoomed in and out, identifying and documenting the limbs and backbone, kidney and brain, mouth and nose that were suddenly, frighteningly human.

"Incredible." Andrew kept shaking his head. When he came home from work that night, the first thing he said was, "That was an amazing morning, babe." The pregnancy was getting more real for both of us. It was like we still weren't used to the idea that there was an actual baby growing inside of me. That we were going to be parents. Life kept chugging along like normal, but soon it was going to be unlike anything we had ever imagined.

We had started a Sunday-night ritual. We'd get into bed, and Andrew would pull out the bestselling pregnancy tome *What to Expect When You're Expecting*. He'd place his hand on my belly, which was now convex even when I was lying down, with a contented smile. "Up the fruit chain," he would say as the book breaks down the development and growth by the week, relaying the size of the fetus to a fruit or vegetable. Our baby girl evolved from a blueberry to a kiwi to a grapefruit, as she developed eyelids and fingernails, and started sucking her thumb, getting the hiccups, and taking naps, all while I blithely rode back and forth on the subway, typing away on my computer, going about daily life.

"Just rest your hand right there," I told Andrew one of those nights as we read in bed. So he did, placing his left his hand on the bottom part of my belly where I had directed. We both laid there, quiet for a minute. Then Andrew jumped.

"Did you feel it?" I asked.

"Oh my God! That's so weird!"

I had just started feeling her move—first, little blips that felt like the ping of carbonation against a can of club soda and then more definitive thrusts against my skin. Andrew had just felt one of those thrusts. "That was her moving?" Andrew asked. "Do you feel that all the time?"

"I'm starting to. Pretty weird, isn't it?" We were both laughing. It was all so insane: three years ago, we were strangers to each other. Then we met, online of all places. Now we had built a home together and there was a little person that we had created growing inside of me.

"Weird." Andrew kissed me tenderly. "And wonderful."

When I turned out the light to go to bed, I couldn't help but think how apropos it all was—my nontraditional love story: wonderful and weird.

THE OVER-
THE-TOP
ICE CREAM
SCENE

Everyone screams for ice cream. Especially artisanal, small-batch, wild, and eccentric ice cream. As this new generation of scoop shops attest, Ample Hills was really on the forefront of a big boom.

In 2009, a Big Gay Ice Cream truck started cruising Manhattan. It offered creations like the Bea Arthur, vanilla soft serve with dulce de leche and crushed Nilla Wafers, and the salty pimp, vanilla soft serve with dulce de leche, chocolate dip, and sea salt. In the fall of 2011, Big Gay partners Douglas Quint and Bryan Petroff opened their first of three brick-and-mortar shops in the city and continue to do awesome philanthropic work for the LBGTQ community through the business.

Former pastry chef Sam Mason opened OddFellows in Williamsburg with two business partners in 2013 and has since developed upwards of two hundred ice cream flavors. Many aren't for the faint of heart: chorizo caramel swirl, prosciutto mellon, and butter, to name a few. Good thing there are saner options in the mix like peanut butter & jelly, s'mores, and english toffee.

A retro scoop shop off the Bowery, Morgenstern's Finest Ice Cream has been bringing fanciful flavors to mature palates since opening in 2014. Creator Nicholas

Morgenstern, who hails from the restaurant world, makes small batches of elevated offerings as Strawberry Pistachio Pesto, Lemon Espresso, and Vietnamese Coffee.

Ice & Vice hails from the Brooklyn Night Bazaar in Greenpoint, and owners Paul Kim and Ken Lo brought it to the Lower East Side in 2015. Another shop devoted to quality small batches, along with weird and wacky flavors, you'll find innovations like Farmer Boy, black currant ice cream with goat milk and buckwheat streusel, and Movie Night, buttered popcorn–flavored ice cream with toasted raisins and chocolate chips.

CHAPTER 9

It's Not a Party
without Cake

It. Was. Amazing.

Whenever anyone had said their wedding was the best day of their life, I thought they were just being dramatic. But as I lounged on the soft white beaches of Saint Bart's in the days following our wedding, I found it hard to disagree. Our wedding was a weekend of overwhelming emotion, celebration, and bliss. I had never felt so loved, honored, and excited—so certain about exactly where I was and what I was doing with my life.

In the end, Andrew and I managed to steer clear of many industry norms and surprised our guests with choices like my navy-blue bridesmaid dress instead of a traditional bridal gown and, in lieu of a sit-down dinner, plying everyone with mini lobster rolls and barbecue sliders in honor of our Connecticut and Kansas City roots. We created a ceremony that replaced religion with what's most meaningful to us: family. Our parents and siblings gave speeches as the foundation of our ceremony, and they were the most incredible words ever spoken. AJ gave an amazing opening speech and Andrew's brother, Dustin, officiated. Andrew and I wrote and recited our own vows to each other. Grown men cried. We let good food, booze, and music do the rest, everyone dancing until midnight with a full moon illuminating Manhattan's skyline outside. And at the end of it all, holy cow, I was a married woman!

Here's how it all went down:

The venue: The space at the New Museum was essentially a modern white box overlooking the downtown skyline. The new Freedom Tower and century-old Woolworth Building, along with the Brooklyn, Manhattan, and Williamsburg Bridges over the East River and all the myriad office towers and apartment buildings with their iconic water tanks in between were visible from the floor-to-ceiling windows. The Empire State and Chrysler Buildings could be seen from the wraparound balcony. We added some cocktail tables and chairs inside and outside, a few floral arrangements, and called the decorations done.

The ceremony setup: There was no wedding aisle or pomp and circumstance. We had everyone come to the museum for happy hour. Guests simply stepped out of the oversized elevators and into a room full of friends, family, and the shadows of the setting sun outside. After about an hour, Dustin graciously ushered everyone together in the center of the room and welcomed them before ceding the mic to AJ.

The speeches: In addition to having Dustin officiate, we had AJ, my mom, dad, and brother, Chris, and Andrew's mother all share their words, thoughts, and memories. It was the best part of the whole wedding.

AJ: Plagued by a certain level of insecurity in high school and college, AJ was a changed woman after getting her MBA and moving to Germany. There, she launched her career as a leadership development coach, traveling to such places as Moscow and Vienna to train C-level executives in how to be more effective in their jobs. In other words, she's now a powerful and self-assured speaker. Even knowing that, having witnessed her transformation throughout the years, I was blown away.

Without any notes, totally calm, poised, and beautiful, AJ walked among the gathering, offering an ode to our thirty years of friendship. She spoke about how our lives have paralleled each other since meeting in junior high and how much richer they are as a result. She brought Andrew in bit by bit, sharing small but pivotal moments like when we played cards with her mom and grandma, and how Andrew impressed them all with his cleverness and smarts—as a bona fide card-shark. "And did you see that hair?" she asked more than once to cheers all around.

My mom: A born-and-raised Yankee, my mom was not the kind of parent who tried to be your best friend, asking who was dating whom, where friends were going to college, how everyone was getting along. She's warm and polite, thoughtful beyond belief, but she's generally reserved, especially in group settings, so I was a bit nervous about her speaking before all the guests. I shouldn't have been—she nailed it.

Again, without any notecards—in fact, no one used notes, which is mind boggling—Mom shared her journey about having had Chris forty-five years earlier, knowing from the moment she found out she was pregnant that it was a boy. But she didn't know when she was pregnant with me. Even after the nurses in the labor room told her it (I) was a girl, she didn't believe them because she had wanted a girl so badly. She was so, so happy, and as I got older and started walking about, she was so excited to have her little princess to dress up in pink ruffles and Mary Janes, but I wouldn't have it. I went wherever Chris went. I followed him and insisted on wearing the same work boots he did because I loved and admired him so. It was the story of motherhood made sweeter knowing that I was pregnant with a girl.

My brother: Fittingly, Chris came next and, with restrained tears after my mom's speech, confessed that the admiration and respect with which I always looked at him had at some point flipped; I was now the one he admired and respected. He said throughout my twenties and thirties, he always knew this day would come, when I would have found my match, someone to make me happy—as he knew Andrew did.

Andrew's mom: A warm, charismatic woman whom everyone always loves after one conversation, including me, Mary Jo gave a wonderful speech about how everyone thinks their child is "special"—but Andrew really is. She spoke proudly and lovingly about Andrew's steady and sure path through life, his unique intelligence and compassion, and that the two of us doing what we love together truly brings out the best in him.

My dad: Wrapping up the family portion of the ceremony, my dad, always good for some laughs, shared his inside joke that Andrew is actually "Prince Andrew," covertly protecting a sprawling estate in Great Britain, complete with royal heritage and family crest. Then turning to proud-papa mode, he recounted how I've always exceeded his expectations academically and career-wise, moving to San Francisco on a whim after college and then giving all of that up to move to New York, doing it again to move to Paris, and now look where we were.

The ceremony itself: "Who we love is a mystery," Dustin said. "Trusting that love is a choice." Dustin took the time to understand the path of Andrew and I coming together and wrote a beautiful ceremony. Filled with honesty and tenderness, weaving in many themes and memories, he recognized not just our love for each other but the importance of our friends and family. "This day, this moment, their wedding is their time to pause, be thankful, and celebrate with the people they love." Amen.

The vows: It was incredible how well the vows that Andrew and I wrote paralleled each other. We both emphasized our admiration and respect for each other and how being together makes each of us, and our lives, so much more complete. Andrew choked up near the end of reading his, and afterward, everyone kept saying how they cried—if it wasn't Andrew who got them, it was one of the others. I couldn't agree more.

The videographer: My one regret is not having hired a videographer or tasking someone with recording that ceremony. It was seriously the most beautiful thing, more moving and meaningful than I ever could have hoped for. And except for the few notes I took to remember the night by, it's all gone.

The dress: In the end, I wore a strapless navy bridesmaid dress. Teenagers today wear fancier dresses to their proms and probably try on ten times as many as I did. But I never saw myself in a billowy ball gown or body-con sheath. Shades of white and cream do nothing for my fair and freckled skin. The only gown I've ever coveted is a navy-and-white-striped Oscar de la Renta original that was once on the cover of *InStyle* magazine—not remotely in my price range even if I could track one down. Besides, you just have to wear what feels natural and what you feel fabulous in, and a navy-blue bridesmaid dress did it for me.

The music: Our music was all over the place, in the best way possible. When guests first arrived at the museum, jazz was playing. But not just any jazz—it was Russ Long, Andrew's uncle who was a well-known composer, singer, and pianist back in Kansas City before passing away in 2006. For our first dance, Andrew and I chose "At Last," to acknowledge our late-in-life meeting, and opted for Beyoncé's rendition to bring a modern edge to the Etta James classic.

From then on, it was a full-on dance fest. From Blondie to Rihanna, Phoenix to Journey, the Cure to Jay Z, we broke out the hits, with everyone young and old representing. My ten-year-old niece did the running man in the middle of a dance circle, Andrew's parents made the Pointer Sisters look cool, my dear friend from San Francisco did a solo performance to Spandau Ballet's "Gold," and Chris, Dustin, and seemingly every other guy on the floor broke out their fiercest air guitar. But I was perhaps most impressed by my new husband, who busted out dance moves even I'd never seen before, slaying us all with his hip-hop style.

The food: As we had known, food matters. But what didn't matter was that our wedding wasn't a traditional sit-down dinner. From zucchini fritters to beet-cured salmon; grilled sea bass with preserved lemon and herbs to rib eye with *salsa verde*; farro with peas, mint and ricotta salata, and tricolor beets with greens and walnuts, plus boards of cheese, charcuterie, and crudités, there was a beautiful abundance of our favorite kinds of food. No one went hungry.

The dessert: There was a lot of pressure on me, as a sweet freak, to have kickass dessert at our wedding. I was as confident in our caterer's desserts as I was everything else, and they didn't disappoint: salted caramel whoopie pies, mini rhubarb galettes, fudgy brownies dusted with sea salt, and tart little pies of lemon curd and blueberry. But still…we had to do something more. As Julia Child said, "A party without cake is just a meeting."

Since our wedding fell on the same weekend as Father's Day, along with the birthdays of my brother, a cousin, and a good friend, we ordered a couple party cakes from Momofuku milk bar. These cakes, as expected, were absurd. One was a birthday cake, vanilla rainbow cake slathered with vanilla frosting and chock-full of crunchy rainbow-cake crumbs. The other more "manly" cake was salted pretzel, baked in stout, burnt honey, and crushed pretzels. Both were over-the-top, ridiculously delicious, and brought me back to other heavenly Momofuku moments.

In 2008, milk bar opened around the corner from my apartment in the East Village. It was in the back of David Chang's second restaurant, Momofuku Ssäm Bar. Since opening his Noodle Bar four years prior to that, Chang, just in his early thirties, had been celebrated for everything from the loud music he piped in (rock 'n' roll!) to the stark decor (hardwood, hard on bony butts), to his attitude that thumbed conventions and expectations (to say nothing of the richly porky broths and flavors he served up). In short, he was a rock star. He set trends. He changed New York's dining landscape. He made consistently smart and visionary choices—one of them being hiring Christina Tosi.

Christina was a graduate of the French Culinary Institute, and had worked at two of Manhattan's more acclaimed restaurants, Bouley and the now shuttered wd-50. She was young, talented, passionate, and doing what she loved. What more could she ask for as a hungry, twentysomething pastry chef than to join a team that fostered her obsession with such junk food as Lucky Charms, maraschino cherries, yellow cake, sour cream potato chips, rainbow sprinkles, mini-marshmallows, gummy bears, Doritos, strawberry jam, pepperoni pizza, and Ovaltine?

When David hired Christina, he gave her what was essentially a laboratory in which to experiment. She exhibited relentless drive and creativity, making my sweet tooth—anyone's, for that matter—look like child's play. After all, this is what she had been doing, eating, and dreaming about her whole life: whipping up crazy concoctions like crack pie, a densely sweet-and-salty pie that sits within an oat cookie crust, and compost cookies, which cram chocolate chips, butterscotch chips, pretzels, potato chips, and coffee grinds into one beautiful, buttery mass of goodness. She is unrepentant about using things like shortening, glucose, and corn syrup. Unapologetic about the copious quantities and varieties of sugar in her recipes. She radiates manic glee when she talks about baking. ("Of course I wanted a bakery when I grew up," she said in a *New York Times* interview. "It's the other little-girl dream besides being a princess.") For Christina, sweets aren't sacred; they are not meant to be precious. They are *fun*.

Some of her creations, like the compost cookie, turned up for the restaurant family meals that she baked for at Momofuku. She also created Ssäm Bar's first dessert, a buttery shortcake with Tristar strawberries, as well as the Noodle Bar's soft-serve ice cream, which went on to become another of her signatures: cereal milk soft serve, which tastes like the sweet milk left at the end of a bowl of cereal. With all the experimentation and collaboration organically happening between Christina and David, they decided to launch Momofuku's next extension together: milk bar.

When milk bar opened around the corner from me, Ben and I went for Breakfast Club, our informal, semi-regular get-togethers that brought us everywhere from the Four Seasons to Doughnut Plant to Clinton Street Baking

Company for such nutritious ways to start the day as french toast with "Nutella bologna" and bananas foster pancakes. This Breakfast Club was a little different. milk bar was brand new and under the radar. We sat in the empty bakery space on a weekday morning—probably the only time milk bar was ever empty in all its history; it didn't take long for lines to start forming out the door—and I think we had some biscuits or breakfast buns. I strangely can't remember. My memory of the experience was eclipsed by the cookies.

There were five of them. The corn cookie had that lovely melty, buttery corn flavor of a quality corn muffin. The blueberry and cream was sweet and crunchy, like a fresh-from-the-oven muffin top. The double chocolate was exactly that: twice the heart-stopping dark richness. The compost cookie was bitter, sweet, salty, crunchy and chewy. And my favorite was the cornflake marshmallow: a chewy, sticky-sweet, crunchy collision of textures and flavors. Every one of the cookies was warm and weeping with butter. Every one of them was a bit deviant. "I *love* unexpected flavor combos," Christina enthuses. "They always make sense in my head, though not always in others'." But these cookies made sense; they made perfect sense to both Ben and me as we annihilated them at the ripe hour of 8:00 a.m.

Just like David, Christina went on to conquer the city, and it's her attitude and warmth as much as anything that has earned her incredible success. She has always been true to her love for home baking. She has never shied away from traditionally frowned-upon ingredients. She is not afraid to fail; she just goes for it. This passion has resulted in seven milk bars in the city, along with Toronto, DC, and Vegas. She has written two cookbooks, received two James Beard awards, and has been a judge on *MasterChef* and *MasterChef Junior*. Her milk bar cookie and cake mixes are sold across the country, and she's constantly appearing in magazines and newspapers. The world loves her. I love her. It made perfect sense to "invite" her to our wedding by way of her party cakes.

"The birthday cake almost seemed like a bad idea at first glance," Christina admits, but then continues: "I grew up on boxed Funfetti cake and consumed canned sprinkle frosting into my college years, but who else *really* loves it that much?! Is it too obvious? Not obvious enough? Too close to the processed, grocery-store specialty? Not something folks will relate to? Turns out, I have a world of vanilla-scented, rainbow-sprinkle-loving, birthday-cake-fanatic soul mates."

Indeed, there are birthday cake soul mates out there in the world. There really are soul mates.

The memory: It was such an amazing night. I remember dusk changing the sky from yellow to orange to purple, and everyone toasting with prosecco. A full moon rose over the Woolworth Building and Freedom Tower, and we danced and danced. Fireworks shot up over Chinatown, and the room got louder and darker and crazier. Andrew and I reveled in all these beautiful, fun, generous people who had come together *for us*. In every photo, I had a shit-eating grin on my face or I was laughing. There are a few when I was crying. I was always beaming.

The takeaway: Fuck the rules! It's your wedding. Wear anything you want, say your vows where you want, and do what you can to appease everyone while remaining true to yourself. Just remember, not everything is going to go exactly according to plan. But even with imperfections, your wedding will be perfect.

THE ULTIMATE NEW YORK DESSERT TABLE

If we had thrown a "dream" wedding, I would have created a fantasy dessert table with anything and everything I love in the city. It would have included the very same Momofuku party cakes that we did have, along with all the other sweets mentioned in this book. And because you can never have too much of a good thing, I would have also added just a few more things.

Peanut butter cookies from Birdbath, an offshoot of City Bakery with locations all over the city. These cookies are like little scoops of fresh peanut butter, baked to a perfect crunch. They're moist and dense, not hard or crumbly, and pack plenty of peanuty sweetness.

I'm a sucker for cream-laden breads, so we would have had Jack Daniels bread pudding from Dessert Club, ChikaLicious in the East Village. As any worthy bread pudding should be, it's dense and eggy with a sweet glaze and boozy punch.

I think a modest selection of malt balls and gummies from Sugar Shop in Carroll Gardens would have been in order too, given the many times Andrew and I stopped there on our urban treks. Besides, who doesn't love a little candy to fuel their night?

And in honor of AJ, her favorite in the city: banana cupcakes from Billy's Bakery. They're soft, fluffy and flavorful with a nice savory cream cheese frosting. I'd also add cupcakes from a few of my other favorite spots: Butter Lane (both the chocolate caramel and the strawberry), Sugar Sweet Sunshine (chocolate with chocolate almond buttercream), and Sweet Revenge (peanut butter with ganache, Mexican vanilla, and raspberry red velvet).

CHAPTER 10

I'll Take a Manhattan

"Y ou're living my dream!" Sandra, the nurse at my
obstetrician's office smiled at me, both conspirato-
rially and shyly.

"Oh?" I wasn't sure what she meant. I had never met her
before and therefore wasn't sure how to respond. I was just
there getting tested for gestational diabetes—not exactly
living the dream.

She surged on, putting the band around my arm to take
my blood pressure. "I'll be forty-one next month, and I'm
trying to get pregnant."

"Oh, awesome!" I told her, my initial hesitation immediately replaced with affection and empathy.

As Sandra entered my vitals into the computer, she continued to pump me with compliments. "I saw that this is your
first child, and you just look amazing! You look like you're

thirty-five!" This woman, a stranger three minutes ago, was totally making my day. "Are you going to have more?" she asked and then continued without giving me a chance to answer. "Say yes. You've got to. That's the only way you know you'll be taken care of when you're older." She went on to share that she was the oldest of eight children. When her grandmother was ailing in her eighties, she and her siblings all took turns housing and caring for her. It was a beautiful and compelling argument, one which I'd heard before, to have multiple kids so there's no pressure on your child to look after you later in life. And because Sandra was so earnest and optimistic, I didn't have the heart to tell her the truth: that Andrew and I were most likely holding at one. We knew we were already lucky to have gotten this far, and we were content with the prospect of having just one child. It's not a popular choice—people don't seem to understand the concept of one and done—but Andrew and I felt comfortable that it was right for us.

But that day, there was no need to dash anyone's hopes. I believed she would get pregnant, she believed I might have more babies, and we both felt a bit uplifted at the end of my appointment.

So six months in, I was doing pretty great. Fast-forward a couple months, and a different story was emerging. I was still pretty lucky—summer's end was approaching, and I was mobile and energetic enough to work out a few times a week and cycle through the same few sets of maternity outfits I'd been wearing in steady rotation. But otherwise my body was starting to rebel.

My ankles had swelled to cankles, I battled hemorrhoids and heartburn, I peed myself every time I sneezed, and I got woozy when I thought about labor. My back and hips ached, I could feel my rib cage expanding, and indeed, if I stayed still, I could literally sense my skin stretching and my insides shifting, trying to accommodate this little person inside me. My own body suddenly seemed too small for my organs, giving me pains and cramps like when you wear tights or pants that squeeze your middle for hours, making you gassy and cranky. I got wicked Charlie horses in the middle of the night, and the general fatigue from hauling around an extra fifteen pounds started wearing me out. It was getting harder to bend over to put on underwear or pet Milo, and whenever I washed my face or brushed my teeth, I left pools of water all over the bathroom floor because my bowling ball of a belly prevented me from getting close to the sink. Emotionally, I might have wanted to drag out the pregnancy forever, but physically, it was time to have this baby.

The discomfort lit a fire under my butt—or maybe it was just the hemorrhoids—but here we were approaching the end of the pregnancy, and we still had tons of stuff to do. We'd been in a blissful dream mode for months, talking about what to name our baby, whether we should take a babymoon, and when to go to all our favorite restaurants while we still had the freedom to do so. But now that she was the size of a large cabbage according to *What to Expect*, we had to prepare for the imminent onslaught. We had to enroll in some birthing and newborn-care classes so we could at least let pretend to know what we were doing when the baby arrived. We still needed to transform our second bedroom, which had enjoyed a brief life as an office, into a nursery. And perhaps the most daunting bit: we had to register, as friends were hosting a baby shower, and we had no idea that we needed.

All along, well-intentioned friends who were new parents gave us books about sleep training, pureeing baby food, and reading newborns' facial expressions. I welcomed anything that might enlighten me as I stepped toward this new phase in life, but these guides felt premature. I didn't even know that it was necessary to train a baby to sleep or when you were supposed to transition from breast milk to actual food. It was hard to appreciate why I'd devote valuable hours reading about what a furrowed forehead meant when I didn't even know what she looked like yet. It was the same with registering: How were we supposed to know what items to request when we had no idea what we were in for? Besides, I thought, how much could a newborn really need?

Then one of Andrew's colleagues gave us a spreadsheet that was both enlightening and terrifying. Within this document's many cells were the brand names, details, pros, and cons of all the baby gear ever created. It included diaper bags and diaper genies, booties and caps, bottles and nipples, nursing pumps and pillows, bath slings and soaps, burp cloths and swaddle blankets, sleep sacks and snuggies, swings and slings, video monitors and wipe warmers, activity mats and bouncers, snot catchers and toenail clippers, to say nothing of car seats and strollers, some of which cost four figures and all of which came in infinite varieties and required hours of analyzing their sizes, attributes, and functions and seemed to require an engineering degree once we got them. Registering was supposed to be fun, but once we realized how little we knew about any of that stuff, it proved to be one of the most stressful parts of the pregnancy.

Even as we became increasingly informed of the enormity of our changing lives, we were still inundated with questions and choices that left us baffled. We browsed online and went to a couple baby stores, picked our friends' brains, and emailed questionnaires, and at the end of it all, I still wasn't entirely sure what the difference was between a Pack 'n Play and a Co-Sleeper. Did a glider really have more soothing capabilities than the oak rocking chair I had managed to hold on to during the move, the one my mom sat in with me when I was a baby? Were we cheap and already bad parents if we bought a crib at Ikea instead of the thousand-dollar models at Giggle, the baby boutique? What did people do before all this gear was invented, anyway?

Along with the research being passed along from newly minted parents, we were accruing all kinds of hand-me-downs. We had stacks of hand-crocheted blankets and sweaters; a new library of baby books to complement the parenting guides; and lots of large, brightly colored plastic objects that required packs of batteries. To top it all off, my mom, the ultimate bargain shopper, had already amassed a wardrobe that would take this girl to her fifth birthday in style. As all this stuff was gifted to us, piles of loosely organized items accumulated in corners around the apartment without anywhere to put them. The pristine, spacious post-renovations feel that we had enjoyed for not even a year was slowly sliding out of our grasp. It was the preview of all the things we would lose control over in our very near future.

God, I missed cocktails.

In some ways, I had been pretty lenient with my diet during pregnancy. A couple glasses of wine per week and the occasional unpasteurized cheese had crossed my lips. I took a relatively relaxed approach to my health, which was fully supported by my obstetrician. But from the list of foods to avoid during pregnancy, there were three that I dutifully abstained from: sushi (tough), raw cookie dough (really tough), and hard alcohol (really, really tough).

In all truthfulness, eschewing cookie dough was probably the worst (the raw eggs in the batter could have salmonella). I mean, what's the point of making cookies if you can't eat the dough along the way? I simply put an embargo on baking rather than deal with the temptation.

But not having a cocktail wasn't so much forgoing the taste as it was missing the experience. It wasn't just deprivation; it was inconvenient. Andrew and I spent a lot of time around the city, relaxing over drinks. It was fun and sexy. A moment to pause and feel the day's needs and stresses slip away while the night unspooled before us. Whether we were uptown or downtown, Manhattan or Brooklyn, in a bar or at a restaurant, it was sublime to feel the alcohol, sip by sip, unknot my shoulders, while Andrew's hand rested on my thigh. Having a cocktail was a small luxury. It was a ritual that I loved. Going out for drinks made me feel connected, young, and relevant. And at a gorgeous bar like Bemelmans, it could make me feel like a million bucks.

Located inside the posh Carlyle Hotel on the Upper East Side, Bemelmans is named in honor of the iconic illustrator Ludwig Bemelmans, whom we would eventually associate with the classic Madeline children's book series. In 1947, he was commissioned by the bar to paint murals depicting the four seasons in Central Park. In exchange, he received two rooms at the hotel for a year and a half for he and his family. The cheeky murals—mustachioed balloon vendors; ice-skating elephants; rabbits on their hind legs, coolly leaning against trees—are now legendary, covering every inch: on the walls, behind the bar, along the columns, even the petite lampshades on each cocktail table and the larger shade on the Steinway grand, where a piano man croons classics like "Fly Me to the Moon" and "What a Wonderful World" every night of the week, are covered with the whimsical art.

I first went to this art deco bar with my dad when he was visiting shortly after I moved to the city. We sat in the warmly lit room on a cold autumn afternoon, "dining" on the mixed nuts, thick parmesan chips, and regular potato chips that filled a trio of silver dishes on the table and which were, more than once, discreetly replenished by one of the gentleman servers. We sipped cocktails slowly, people watching from a prime table along the wall, to delay returning to the bitter outdoors—and just to prolong the wonderful experience of being transported to a time when simple pleasures and manners mattered. As bar manager Javier Martinez says, Bemelmans "is like traveling in time. Guests still want to experience the New York that everyone fell in love with decades ago."

Somewhere along the line, the luxe bar had become the place for me and Andrew to go whenever we wanted something just a little out of the ordinary. It didn't have to be a birthday or anniversary; it could just be the craving for something exceptional, to feel like we were in a Woody Allen movie for the night. The lighting is sublime. There are corners for canoodling. There's a hushed merriment beneath the fourteen-karat-gold-covered ceiling. "It's the essence of New York," as Javier says.

It can be especially tough to get a table in the winter months, when guests are inclined to linger as my dad and I had. Everyone loves Bemelmans. There are rotund old men with shiny domes and bifocals, dandy Europeans in jackets and velvet slippers, and gaggles of uptown ladies sporting head-to-toe Vuitton or Hermés along with their taut arms, leathery tans, and faces full of injectables. You'll see ascots and furs, emeralds and walking sticks. "It's like a theater in a way," Javier says of the scene. People near and far—a mix of hotel guests and residents, business tycoons and socialites, neighborhood locals and interlopers like me and Andrew—simply adore being there.

Besides the atmosphere and cocktails, what makes Bemelmans magical are the employees, who have been there for years—or more often, decades. The loyalty bar was set pretty high by the previous head bartender, Tommy Rowles, who retired in 2012 after fifty-three years with Bemelmans. Today there's Luis Serrano who has worked the bar for twenty-three years, Rashid Abdul who's been there for nine, and the only female bartender, Lori Bodinizzo, who has been there a mere four years. The same goes for the waiters. The servers I've most often had are Roger, a portly man from the Bahamas who's coming up on a quarter century of serving cocktails with a gracious smile, and Mario, who's been there for thirty-six years. Every time you go, you can expect to see the same friendly faces—it's like nowhere else in the city.

You can get everything from a mocktail of pineapple juice, ginger beer, and muddled mint, to a $345 taste of 1930 Château de Laubade Armagnac, but ultimately the classics are king. "Guests come for the same martini their aunt had when they were kids," explains Javier. I'm a bit of a wimp when it comes to martinis and their nearly straight pours of gin or vodka. My cocktail of choice used to be a sidecar, a sweet-sour mixture of cognac, Cointreau, and lemon juice served up with a sugared rim. I loved the grit of the sugar granules sliding through my teeth as the smooth, sweet liquid flowed down my throat. But in the years since I had met Andrew, I had firmly switched over to rye manhattans. (Sidecars are fabulous in the moment, I learned, not so much the next day.)

The manhattan's roots are said to go back to 1874, when it was concocted at a banquet at New York City's Manhattan Club for presidential nominee Samuel J. Tilden. Nearly a century and a half later, the cocktail is thriving, with scores of bars putting their own twists on the classic—adding absinthe, apricot brandy, maple syrup, and the like. At Bemelmans, it's simple and pure, made with Carpano "Antica Formula" sweet vermouth, a dash of Angostura bitters, brandied cherries, and the whiskey or rye of your choice. It's exquisitely harmonious: heady, smoky, with a fiery bite that becomes ever so sweet in the aftertaste. You might want to complain about its $27 price tag, but it's about twice the size at Bemelmans as any other bar, and nowhere else serves it with such panache.

I remember one time when Andrew and I sat next to another couple along a banquette. They were playful and affectionate with one another, leaning over the table in intimate, nonstop conversation. He had his hand on hers, and occasionally they would smooch across the table. The thing is, they were both easily in their seventies. And they were still so chic, so cool, and so clearly madly in love, I simply couldn't take my eyes off them.

"That's what I want," I whispered to Andrew, holding his gaze while nodding my head toward the couple as subtly as possible. "When I'm that old, I want to be out and about, having a great time at Bemelmans. I want to still be in love and be affectionate—and be able to handle these cocktails!"

Andrew took my hand and kissed it before entwining his fingers with mine. "Me too." He smiled at me.

I gazed at our neighbors again and then across at Andrew while picking up my manhattan to enjoy the last sip of biting brown liquor and the last brandied cherry at the bottom.

Thinking about this interlude now, it just felt wrong that we couldn't go to Bemelmans and sip manhattans to say farewell to our days of freedom.

For all I had achieved, for all the happiness and gratitude I felt in life, I still found myself contemplating the definition of success. I had always equated it with external recognition: the ad career, moving abroad, publishing articles and books. I just assumed these achievements would keep coming and I would relish their victory along the way. But I now found myself on a new path, one that was more inwardly focused. With getting married and preparing to have a baby, I was more consciously "inside" my life and relationship, rather than out in the world, proving my salt.

I still wasn't freelancing or writing as much, as they required energy I was short on. I didn't go out or see friends as often as I used to or party late into the night. There were so many used-to's and old habits; it made me sad on one hand—but it was also a bit of a relief.

When I lived alone, I devoted so much time to writing, whether it was researching and pitching a new story, blogging, or actually working on an assigned piece. I rarely let myself have a weeknight or weekend day off without some bit of writing and would get noticeably agitated if too many social obligations got in the way. But along with saying *c'est la vie* about my changing body, I was embracing my newer ways and habits. Instead of whooping it up in Manhattan, I loved being home, cooking, puttering, hanging out with "my boys"—Andrew and Milo—waiting for our baby girl to arrive. It was time to be more inwardly directed, to have a smaller world and deeper focus, and to not feel the constant pressure of deadlines and goals. I would always write, I reasoned, just as I'd always cherish the memories of my times in the city with AJ and wax nostalgic about them. But by letting go of what once was, I realized I could move on. I was ready for act two. It would be a whole new adventure and, with a little luck, just as exciting as the one before it.

....

"Are you happy about this?" Andrew asked. "Are you bummed? Are you ready?" His firing of questions was almost a joke between us at this point, the eve of giving birth. We talked often about what we were most nervous and excited about and, yes, what we were going to miss. But there were no easy answers. Most first-time parents will tell you: you're never truly ready. As happy as you are, as much as your heart and soul are in it, your experience of adulthood is going to change forever.

After twenty years of being independent, it wasn't going

to be about me or my life anymore. It wasn't even going to be so much about Andrew, the man it took me years to find. It would be about sustaining this baby's life: going through the motions of feeding, bathing, and comforting her for the first few months until she was big enough to start engaging, then walking and talking, then becoming independent herself. There was no way of knowing what parenthood would be like or what surprises lay ahead. But I was definitely happy, not bummed, and I was about to find out if I was ready.

THE CITY'S
BEST CLASSIC
HOTEL BARS

A year after moving there, I had rekindled my love for Brooklyn, enjoying the borough's smaller-scale bars and restaurants and overall laid-back vibe. But if there is one thing Manhattan has over Brooklyn, it's historic five-star hotels. And inside these hotels are some of the most divine (and divinely expensive) places to cocktail.

Featuring a Maxfield Parrish mural of Old King Cole, a "merry old soul," that was originally painted in 1906 and moved to the King Cole Bar inside the St. Regis when the luxe hotel opened in 1932, this Midtown bar is similar to Bemelmans—but different. Higher ceilings, a smaller space, and a more suit-and-tie crowd give it a decidedly stately feel.

Whereas Bemelmans and the King Cole Bar are especially lovely in the fall and winter, when you might want to sit in a dark, posh corner for hours, the Peninsula's Salon de Ning is perfect in the summertime, or at that first crack of spring. It's a simple, sophisticated rooftop bar on the twenty-third floor, which feels very far from its Midtown location.

Perched high over Columbus Circle and Central Park, the thirty-fifth floor Lobby Lounge at the Mandarin

Oriental is especially magical at dusk. Even if you don't score one of the tables along the floor-to-ceiling windows, the dramatic views of treetops and skyscrapers can be seen from nearly every seat.

For a different flavor of decadence, head downtown to the bright and poppy Crosby Street Hotel in SoHo. Massive paintings, textured upholstery, and eclectic fixtures abound, along with posh drinks and tea.

Then Comes Baby and the $1,000 Carriage

PART 3

Then Comes Baby and the $1,000 Carriage

CHAPTER 11

All Hail the Kale Salad

H ello, miss, your car is here." It was Wednesday, October 8, 2014. Three years (minus fifteen days) since I had met Andrew, one year since we had moved in together, four months since we'd gotten married, and now there was a car and driver waiting downstairs to take us to the hospital. So we could have a baby. *We were having our baby.*

It was a glorious day of cerulean-blue skies and starburst-yellow sunshine. Thanks to New York's Indian summer, I had only had to buy one season of maternity clothes, making the same army jacket I wore that spring still work over my ruched maternity top, so long as I didn't try zipping it. I couldn't wait to ditch the little maternity garb I did have. Even though my sartorial future of old-man pajama sets and beater sweats was hardly sexy, I was sick of the same elastic-waist jeans and shapeless dresses I had been cycling through for months.

Outside the Town Car's windows, I watched the bodegas, Thai restaurants, and seventies-era dry cleaners of Flatbush Avenue go by. We passed Franny's and Sharlene's, the money trap we'd nearly bought two years earlier, then Barclays Center, where I had yet to see a Nets game or big-headliner concert. Then the Brooklyn Academy of Music, the nation's oldest performing arts center, where Andrew and I had gone to NPR performances, jazz concerts, archival movies, and Q&As with directors that summer in a frantic effort to do everything we could before having a baby. We had practically binged on culture, almost more than restaurants, knowing our imminent opportunities would be few and far between. At least we had managed a few last hurrahs—the Angelika and Arturo's, one of our favorite Friday night movie-and-pizza combos; dark and tranquil dinners at the Waverly Inn in the West Village and Rucola in Boerum Hill; and weekends away in Boston and the sticks of Pennsylvania. Now, the phone in my lap kept beeping and buzzing, friends and family members texting us good luck and well wishes for Delivery Day. I felt like a soldier going off to battle, with the troops anxiously on standby.

It was a long journey to the hospital on the Upper East Side where, inexplicably, my obstetrician who practiced in Brooklyn Heights, delivered. As we drove uptown, I was heading toward a new future, and outside the windows, the city played like my own mini-farewell-tour.

The Houston Street exit reminded me of all the taxis that had sped downtown to deliver me at some bar—Barramundi, Pravda, Chloe 81—to meet friends. I gazed at the East River promenade, where Andrew and I had enjoyed watching Chinese fishermen and teenage basketball players on a long Sunday stroll. Past the East Village, and the countless dates, drinks, and nights spent dancing in dark rooms throughout my thirties. Murray Hill, or "Curry Hill," which brought back all the cheap Indian takeout I had overindulged in while living there when I first moved to the city as a twenty-nine-year-old whippersnapper. Speeding onward through Midtown, I recalled being a kid and tagging along with my dad when he had jobs in the city and the wonder I felt when visiting the World Trade Center and the American Museum of Natural History and shopping at Fiorucci and Rizzoli. This city and me: we ran deep.

Forty minutes later, we pulled up to the hospital's Fifth Avenue entrance. Andrew grabbed my bag filled with cheap granny underwear and button-up pajamas, the must-have items mom friends and guidebooks had insisted were important. They'd be comfortable enough to wear after my C-section and accessible to a newborn's nursing needs. More to the point, they could be tossed once they were bloodied. I was lucky enough that I'd never had any kind of surgery, so I didn't know what to expect, but apparently copious amounts of blood were going to be gushing from me for weeks and I'd never again want to see, much less wear, the soiled clothes.

After checking in at the front desk, Andrew and I were escorted to the recovery room, where we'd wait two hours for our turn in the OR. Two of the three other beds were occupied, one by a woman who was indeed recovering, with a brand-new baby suckling her breast. The other, I learned from eavesdropping—not that there was much choice as our beds were five feet apart, separated by cloth curtains and various beeping machines—was also there for a C-section.

According to the Centers for Disease Control, the number of cesarean sections has skyrocketed in America from 4.5 percent when they first started measuring the statistic in 1965 to 32 percent today—or nearly one in every three. *Nearly one in three babies is now delivered by cesarean section.* It's performed more than any other surgery in this country. Like so many other procedures in our healthcare system, it's indicative of the cost of business taking priority over patients' care. Doctors make more money for hospitals by doing C-sections, and they can control their own schedules better. I wanted to rebuke my C-section on principle but, as my mom pointed out, this baby had a mind of her own. She was breech—feet first instead of headfirst, as is necessary for a vaginal delivery—so it would be a C-section for me. I got over it pretty quickly. As all my friends pointed out—seven of the eight girlfriends at my baby shower had C-sections, so the real statistic may even be higher than what's recorded—there are serious benefits to knowing exactly when you'll be delivering and bringing a newborn home. You get to stay in the hospital longer and a surgical incision in the belly is arguably less traumatic than tearing your cooch from pushing too hard.

As I stripped down and put on the hospital-issued gown made with coarse cotton and socks with little traction treads, Andrew tried to look relaxed on a fold-out chair in our teeny slice of the frenetic room. "Hi, my name is Dr. Lee and I'll be doing your anesthesia today," said a tall Asian guy, probably half my age but with confidence beyond my years, after he ducked into our tented section with a reassuring smile. He explained how my spinal would be administered, asked if I had questions, and then was gone. He was just one of several doctors and nurses who rotated in and out over the next couple hours, prepping me: taking my vitals, asking about my medical history, double- and triple-checking about any known allergies. I was calm throughout it all except when the first IV went in and I nearly passed out, as I'm wont to do.

"Okay," a nurse said, pulling back the curtain. "Andrew, you're going to stay here. These are your scrubs and mask. Put them on, and someone will come get you in about fifteen minutes. Amy." She turned to me. "Are you ready?"

Andrew and I looked at each other with a shared expression: *Holy crap!*

"All right, babe." I kissed my husband beneath the florescent lights. "I'll see you in there."

The next ninety minutes were an out-of-body experience. After being injected in my spine with a cocktail of drugs to numb my lower body, I was reclined to a horizontal position, crucifix style, my arms stretched out on either side of me. A screen was hung between my chest and the medical SWAT team assembled on the other side to bring this baby girl into the world. Andrew, behind a face mask, hair cap, and full body suit, sat next to me, whispering encouragement, his face soft and vulnerable.

"How are you doing? Do you feel okay?" Every few minutes a head would pop up over the screen to ensure I was still breathing, but not feeling, as they cut through my skin and muscle tissue, tugging and rooting around inside my abdomen. "You're doing great," they'd tell me as if I were pushing or somehow contributing to this birth.

The minutes ticked slowly. I kept looking between Andrew and the clock, waiting, waiting, licking my dry lips. I was crawling out of my skin, not from the drugs coursing through my veins but in anticipation. I needed to know that our baby girl was okay, that she was healthy and alive—it was clear she was already adorable and determined, as she'd appeared in the 3-D ultrasound print-out I'd been staring at for months, with her fist up near her chin, Rodin's *Thinker*-style.

"I see a foot!" The lead anesthesiologist peeked her head

over the screen, giving me a thumbs-up. Here it was: the final stretch. My ears tuned in to what was happening down there, waiting for that newborn yowl. When I heard it, it wasn't so much a piercing cry as the sweetest little whimper. As soon as I heard it, the tears started flowing. "Is she okay? Is she okay?" Andrew's glasses were fogged up with emotion. And then the cries came. She started wailing, really wailing. The nurse held up this writhing, slimy, pink, impossibly cute baby before quickly ushering her over to a scale beneath a warming lamp. "She looks great! Andrew? Get over here!"

Andrew jumped up, heeding the first call of his brand-new paternal duties. He ceremoniously clamped the umbilical cord and started snapping photos of our screeching seven-pound-four-ounce wonder, returning to my side repeatedly to assure me everything was fine, she looked beautiful. It wasn't until forty-five minutes later, when I was all stitched up and back in recovery, that I finally got to hold my baby girl.

I'm not a religious person but experiencing pregnancy and giving birth changes you. As I stared at this water-logged creature, eyes nearly swollen shut, lips already finding my breast, swaddled tightly into a football of white, blue, and magenta blanket, I could hardly fathom that she had grown from a couple of cells and become someone inside of me. That she was the result of me and Andrew having sex. That his sperm connected with my egg and cells divided again and again and again and again, creating a skeleton and a heart and lungs and eyelids and hair and little fingers and toes and that little tongue that kept poking out of her lips like some alien being. Once again, I was awed by what the human body—a *woman's* body—is capable of doing. That my skin had stretched and internal organs shifted and my own system had provided sustenance, shelter, and life to this new being for months while we talked to her, wondered what she'd look like, who she'd be like, and what we'd name her. It is beyond biblical, beyond science fiction. But it had happened. There she was. There we were. A new family of three.

I admit it now: I was cavalier toward all my friends who had kids in our twenties and thirties. No, I take that back—I was a shit. I didn't give them any credit or even try to appreciate the radical intensity of new parenthood. The sleep deprivation. The upside-down reality. The colossal change of priorities. The helplessness and overwhelming responsibility of it all.

Now that I was being awoken every two hours to nurse the peanut—as we started calling our baby girl—shell-shocked from the cluster feeding that no one had told me about, I got it. And yet, as the coming weeks and months would attest, I was getting only the tiniest tip of it. My world would never be the same again.

Those first days and weeks after the peanut was born were warped bands of time that extended forever and yet were broken down and carefully tracked by the minute: she fed thirteen minutes on the left breast, fourteen on the right; it was sixty minutes since the last feeding; she'd had an eight-minute crying fit and a twenty-minute nap. All this timekeeping of the peanut's eating and sleeping—along with her every pee, poop, fart, hiccup, and scrunched facial expression—was scrupulously recorded in a notebook I kept at my side. I filled three notebooks of cryptic numbers—reminding me, uneasily, of the schizophrenic mathematical genius John Nash from *A Beautiful Mind*—every entry seemingly critical to the peanut's well-being and absolutely essential to my confidence and sanity. So much was riding on my competence and yet—*hel-lo?*—I had no idea what I was doing.

I was afraid I'd break the peanut's arm putting her in a onesie. Afraid I'd snap her neck by holding her incorrectly. Afraid she'd catch a chill and then pneumonia if I brought her outside. Afraid I'd drown her giving her a sponge bath (did you know a baby can drown in a teacup of water?). Afraid I'd fall asleep while nursing her and either drop her from my lap or crush and suffocate her, depending if I was sitting or lying down while doing it. Afraid I'd drop her on our hardwood floors. Afraid Milo would attack her, though, to his credit, he was keeping a curious but detached distance, undoubtedly recognizing that his number-one status in the household had been usurped. I was afraid, afraid, afraid—which I realized was yet another aspect of this new life called parenthood I hadn't been expecting.

Eight days in, as I melted into our living room couch at 2:00 a.m. with the peanut passed out on my chest, I had flashbacks to my sophomore year of college when, in an effort to broaden my social circle, I pledged a co-ed fraternity. For two months, I had been awoken in the early morning hours with hot whiskey shots, taken to a dark basement in the middle of nowhere for no reason, and then would have to resume normal academic and social behavior hours later. Hazing and sleep deprivation—it's no joke, both on college campuses and with newborn babies.

I'd hear the peanut cry in my sleep and get out of bed to feed her only to discover her fast asleep. Or in the middle of the night, while I was on the couch and Andrew slept in our bedroom, I'd witness wild dance parties in our neighbor's apartment. But when I incredulously put my glasses on, I was embarrassed that what I was seeing were plants, not writhing people, in the neighbor's window across the way. It was just like that pledge semester when I'd mildly hallucinate during French class. You go a little mental in the new parenthood bubble.

Aside from sleep deprivation, probably the biggest challenge those first few weeks was breastfeeding. Fraught with anxiety, it raised all kinds of questions, which led to insecurities. Was I doing it right? Was my posture okay? Was I producing enough milk? Where was the milk coming from, anyway? How would I know when to change breasts? How would I know when to stop? Why was she crying? Why did she fall asleep? Should I burp her now? Are these gigantic breasts really *mine*?

Not for nothing, my mom gave me formula when I was a baby. But I was living in a time, in a city, where it was expected that you'd submit to breastfeeding. In Tina Fey's book, *Bossypants*, she refers to all those holier-than-though mothers who look down on other moms who give their babies formula as "Teat Nazis." They consider breastfeeding about the noblest act of motherhood, if not life, and, according to Tina, "Their highest infestation pockets are in Brooklyn and Hollywood." Indeed, I was surrounded by them.

The peanut had a mean latch when it came to breastfeeding, so at least I didn't have to deal with her not latching, which is a common problem for new moms trying to nurse. Every two hours, I'd dutifully pop out one of my breasts, and then the other, so she could feed and my body would keep producing milk. And yet she wasn't gaining weight. My pediatrician had us return every three or four days for a weigh-in and, with each visit, I got progressively more uptight. What was I doing wrong? How could she not be putting on weight? Was I not producing enough milk? My right breast seemed full and abundant, but my left breast less so and the peanut less interested in it. Newborns typically drop a few ounces in the days immediately after birth, but regain it within two weeks. We were now three weeks in and the peanut hadn't regained her birth weight. I was officially freaking out. So what's a new mom embedded amongst Teat Nazis to do? Hire a lactation consultant.

The Friday of my appointment fell on Halloween. As all the other parents in my neighborhood were putting final details on their kids' superhero, princess, and zombie costumes while I stripped to the waist before an utter stranger. "May I touch your breasts?" asked the beaming Trinidadian woman standing directly in front of me, hands paused in midair as if she had been about to cop a feel.

"Sure, of course," I agreed, totally unfazed. Now that I pretty much lived with my breasts hanging out, regardless who might be in the room—friend, father-in-law, neighbor's awkward ten-year-old—what difference did it make if this stranger touched them? And touching them was only the beginning.

For the next four hours, the lactation consultant kindly manhandled me, teaching me different breastfeeding positions—the cradle, cross-cradle, side lying, and football hold—while weighing the peanut along the way as I nursed. Just as it was amazing to see her weight steadily go up ounce by ounce over the course of the afternoon, it was enlightening to under-stand the challenge I was up against. If I was having one or two bad feedings a day, the peanut was losing a half ounce of milk, which is why she wasn't gaining weight. Suddenly, mere ounces had the same urgency in my life as minutes. But this fastidious and optimistic lactation consultant was going to help me figure it out. Her goal that day was to teach me the tips and tricks of baby nutrition and feeding techniques that would make me the ultimate breastfeeder.

It was the first time, but definitely not the last, that I real-ized everything about motherhood is about being the best.

Ordinarily I relish any excuse to drink champagne and eat cake. But with my own birthday landing three weeks after the peanut's arrival, I wasn't whipping up any celebrations that year. And yet it ended up being one of my favorite birth-days ever. After all, I awoke to the smell of warm, buttery pretzel croissants.

While Dominique Ansel has received deserved worldwide publicity for his doughnut-croissant hybrid, the Cronut, the original croissant mash-up gets little fanfare. Maury Rubin of City Bakery developed this signature pastry, a beautiful speci-men of classic handmade French technique made modern, in 1996. The pretzel croissant is tender and flaky, buttery and stretchy, then twisted, not quite so far as a pretzel, but further than your normal croissant. It's then dusted with sesame seeds, giving it its signature look and savory flavor. Andrew had cleverly smuggled in two the night before, warmed them in the oven, and surprised me, serving them on a tray with coffee and tea in the living room when I woke up. It was better than Christmas morning.

After first prolonging the anticipation, admiring the croissants and their flaky skins, and then devouring them, I opened the gifts and cards that Andrew had gotten for me from the peanut even though she, cradled comfortably in my left arm, was clearly my gift. To ensure I remained in a happy place, holed up in the apartment alone all day while he was at work, Andrew also left me with two City Bakery chocolate chip cookies that were slick with creamed butter and sugar and a promise to return in the evening with more treats.

Ten hours later, Andrew appeared with a brown shopping bag containing my birthday dinner. I once again asked myself how I had gotten so lucky to find this man. He had gone to James.

Andrew and I had discovered James, located on a picturesque residential block filled with brownstones with majestic stoops and verdant trees, during our real estate hunt the previous year. In all our Sunday afternoon crisscrossing, we passed the restaurant several times and there were always gobs of people waiting out on the corner for brunch. By the second or third drive-by, we knew we had to check it out. When we finally did—splitting the fluffy ricotta lemon pancakes in blueberry syrup and scrambled eggs with greasy duck sausage, by then happily in our sweet-savory splitting mode at restaurants—we hoped that, if we didn't wind up in Prospect Heights, our future neighborhood would at least have a comparable spot with such awesome food and a warm and chic ambiance.

James had been building its devout following since it opened in 2008. Back then, the neighborhood was more on the cusp, located on the "wrong side" of Flatbush Avenue. The closest main drag for local residents, Vanderbilt Avenue, didn't offer much in the way of sit-down restaurants, much less cozy spots for bourgeoisie burger-and-beer types like us. James changed that.

It had previously been a restaurant called Sorrel, and before that, it was one of the city's thousands of nondescript delis. It resided within a three-story brownstone on a corner lot and the couple who lived in the apartment upstairs, Deborah Williamson and her-then husband, Bryan Calvert, just so happened to be in the market to open a restaurant in Brooklyn. They had been looking for a space for two years, so when Sorrel was closing, they jumped at the opportunity.

Bryan was a chef with six restaurants, including the four-star

Bouley, under his belt. Deborah had a background in magazines and production. They both had a knack for cooking, farming, and design—three altars at which Brooklynites genuflect. It was a no-brainer to open a neighborhood restaurant that would rely on fresh, local ingredients and serve modern comfort food in an understatedly cool atmosphere. When all the paperwork was done, they were more than ready to get in and make the space theirs.

The couple gutted it, restoring original architectural details, including the aged plaster wall behind the bar and pressed tin ceilings. They outfitted the rest with simple, modern touches, painting the brick walls white, installing brown banquettes, and anchoring the modest square dining room with an oversized Plexiglas chandelier. "We wanted a natural, organic feel and to keep its original charm," Deborah explains. It was the same philosophy with the menu. They created one that changed with the seasons and was supplemented by their own eight-hundred-square-foot rooftop herb garden. When James debuted, it was one of the first restaurants to work with farmers and purveyors, offering "seasonal, sustainable, locally inspired" dishes, and it was immediately popular.

Now, kale salads are menu staples at every Brooklyn restaurant worth its farm-to-table credo, but James preceded the trend. Their formative years were dominated by much heartier fare, including bone marrow and sweetbreads, but by 2010, wanting something lighter for herself and sensing a change in collective appetites, Deborah pushed for greener additions. "I wanted to put a kale salad on the menu. I was craving something healthier," she says of the signature dish's early entry. And so Bryan developed the recipe and they introduced it to the world—or at least, the neighborhood— and it stuck. To this day, the kale salad rivals the burger as the most popular item on the menu.

Andrew brought the kale salad home from James, along with their roasted chicken stewing in jus and leeks, and a superrich and buttery pasta flecked with sheets of Swiss chard. We put the peanut in the gargantuan mechanical swing that had overtaken our living room and was the only place she was content to just chill, and popped open some prosecco, my first bottle of booze since giving birth. Then we tore into the brown takeout boxes.

When does a salad trump roasted chicken and creamy pasta? When the kale is finely shredded and tossed with quinoa and smoked almonds before being buried under copious amounts of grated ricotta salata and topped with a perfectly poached farm egg. It was smoky, crunchy, creamy, and savory at once. And, thanks to the added protein of the egg, "You don't feel deprived," as Deborah points out. I crunched through several bites, intent on the mélange of flavors in my mouth and how the bubbles of the prosecco played against them. I definitely didn't feel deprived; I felt totally, utterly indulged. Almost unhinged. As if reading my mind, Andrew clinked my glass and winked at me without a word. Forget all my previous cake-and-champagne-fueled birthdays: *this* was living.

Over the next week, I made three more visits to the pediatrician for weigh-ins, every one of them a big freaking deal. Everything in those first weeks after birth, including journeying six blocks into the outside world, had so many new layers of complications. Yes, I was forty-two now and, yes, I was getting a grip on breastfeeding and, yes, I had kept the peanut alive so far. But I was still wildly intimidated. For a doctor's visit, first, I had to actually get dressed and look presentable and then decide what was temperature appropriate for the peanut to wear. I had to transport her somehow, which meant figuring out all that new gear, with multiple straps and belts and safety latches, and packing her in it with care. I had to organize a bag with all the essentials that she might need: diapers, wipes, a new change of clothes in case of explosive poops, swaddle blankets, burp cloths, plushie toys for distraction, pacifiers to soothe, hand sanitizer, and insurance information for my new dependent. And I had to somehow time her feedings so I could get to the doctor's while she still had full belly and wouldn't break down crying in front of the pediatrician, making me look like an incompetent mom. For someone so tiny, she required *a lot*.

But I did it. I got ready, packed the bag, mastered the gear, and stepped out into the world, and when I did, I saw parents with new eyes. I appreciated the men with babies strapped to and dangling from their torsos for being good partners and doing their parts. But I wanted to bow down and pay respect to all the women. I looked at them pushing strollers—you could always tell the new moms versus the nannies not by the color of their skin but by the wild look of panic in their eyes—and instead of getting annoyed by the space they deigned to take on the sidewalk as I always had, I'd give them a wide berth and an empathetic smile. I had crossed over. I was one of them, a fellow mom, as responsible and emotionally raw as I ever had been in my life. These women and I now shared the same fears and battle scars. We had a unique perspective on the world that started outside ourselves, with someone else. We were kindred spirits.

And finally, four weeks in, after a half dozen treks to the pediatrician, the peanut surpassed her birth weight. The two of us together, minute by minute, ounce by ounce, we were making progress.

ARTISANAL MANIA IN BROOKLYN

Kale, the emblem of Brooklyn food trends, is only the tip of the iceberg. The small batch, organic, hand-crafted, artisanal, hipster foodie scene continues to be alive and well across all imaginable food groups.

The brothers who perhaps best symbolize this Brooklyn food movement, Michael and Rick Mast, started selling their Mast Brothers chocolate bars in 2007 at a flea market and now have factories in Williamsburg, London, and Los Angeles. Wrapped in impeccably designed papers, the bars come in esoteric flavors like smoke, coffee, and goat milk and have probably fetched the brothers gazillions of dollars.

Nekisia Davis was working at Franny's (the pizzeria on Flatbush Avenue) when she started making her own granola on the side. She bagged it and started selling it at Brooklyn Flea, the same flea market where the Brothers Mast—and, for that matter, gobs of other artisanal food makers—started and went on to become the woman behind the granola juggernaut known as Early Bird Granola.

Chef Fany Gerson opened Dough in Bed–Stuy in 2010, and her big, billowy, brioche-style doughnuts have spread across the city and are now available at dozens of third-party locations (including Smorgasburg, which is where we first sampled the bad boys). With delectable flavors like blood orange, hibiscus, and toasted coconut, inspired by Fany's Latin American heritage, to know Dough is to love it.

Naturally, Anarchy in a Jar supports local and family farmers—this is Brooklyn! A lesser credo just wouldn't cut it. The small-batch condiments company was started in 2009 by Laena McCarthy and includes deliciously eclectic offerings like grapefruit & smoked salt marmalade, cherry balsamic jam, and beer mustard.

CHAPTER 12

Pounding Cookies
by the Half Pound

I t's crazy to look back at photos from those first few weeks and see how teeny the peanut was. Once we got through the initial hazing period and the hiccups of breastfeeding, she plumped right up and then became a bona fide chunker. Miraculously, I did not.

I say that because when I finally turned my attention away from the peanut and to myself, I realized I was eating like a truck driver. I'd devour two breakfasts, two lunches, and in the late afternoon be overwhelmed by another wave of hunger so fierce that it sent me to the refrigerator, attacking the hummus and demolishing a sleeve of crackers until the peanut's cries in the other room made me feel guilty enough to put the food down. At dinner, Andrew would be sated—like other well-balanced human beings—with one serving. After having seconds, I found myself feeling self-conscious about wanting thirds, so I'd take cover in the kitchen, ostensibly to do the dishes but really so I could stick my fork in the simmering turkey chili again and again while Andrew and the peanut cuddled in the living room. I couldn't believe how insatiable I was. It was a relief to finally discover that the metabolic demands of breastfeeding require consuming an extra five hundred calories a day, thereby explaining my animallike impulses.

And yet as the weeks went on, I was somehow dropping weight. Even as I got more brazen with my snacking—healthy hummus and almonds soon gave way to all manner of sugary, chocolaty, butter-laden treats—I was within striking distance of my prepregnancy weight. My stomach shrank back toward its previous incarnation. If I tried really hard, I could wiggle into my old jeans. Breastfeeding—I suddenly *loved* it! It gave me license to behave badly—very, very badly.

At first, just due to proximity of my apartment and my own laziness, I'd run to the pharmacy or grocery store and get a bag of M&M's (Pretzel! Peanut butter! Crispy! So many new varieties!). Not the diddly individual-sized bags at checkout, but the big bags that are usually shared among a team at the office. I'd get them home and promptly annihilate them in about an hour's time.

Before long, going out in the afternoon for a snack became the focal point of my day. Not only did it get me out of the apartment, which had become my whole 1,100-square-foot universe, but it also brought me even closer to the peanut. For now that I had figured out how to position all the straps and folds of the carrier, it was my baby gear of choice. I loved "wearing" her, feeling her beating heart against my own as we set off on walks through Brooklyn's sloping streets. The neighborhood was so pretty with all the remaining yellow, red, and golden autumn leaves clinging to the trees and dusting the stoops. Feeling the peanut breathing against me made it all seem ever more romantic—the original vision I'd had of Brooklyn, feeling warm, connected, like I belonged there, was finally mine.

Except now I was like a Neanderthal searching for and bringing meat back to the cave—my meat being *tres leches* doughnuts from Doughnut Plant, berry and almond tarts from Joyce Bakery, and Nutella cookies from Buttermilk Bakery. I didn't even wait to get my haul home—I'd start eating my freshly baked conquest while walking past the perfectly aligned brownstones along one of the quieter side streets, fingers exposed to the brisk air and tingling, my nose red and runny, while my mouth got busy nibbling and licking. I was technically more of adult than ever, and yet I had regressed by any ordinary observation.

I discovered another perk of breastfeeding—besides gluttonously stuffing my maw—was being relegated to the couch for a good chunk of the day. I understand why a lot of women feel trapped and frustrated on maternity leave, being stuck with their breasts out and hands occupied for hours when they're used to kicking ass at the office. But I was more than content with a book, magazine, or crossword puzzle in one hand while I fed the peanut in the other (I had come a long way, mastering the breastfeeding positions the lactation consultant had taught me). And one habit just seemed to enable another. New to Instagram, I started cruising local foodies' feeds, salivating over their posted photos of oozing cinnamon buns, dainty pastel macarons, and perfectly geometric black-and-white cookies. I'd click through a post, discover a profile, stumble upon a website, and fall into these massive Internet rabbit holes that were simultaneously enlightening and frightening. I had New York's entire food-obsessed world at my fingertips. Every day there was a new discovery beckoning me to leave my living room.

This was how I discovered City Cakes, home of the half-pound sugardoodle. I was shocked that in all my days of covering food and sweets for local magazines and newspapers, I hadn't heard of this bakery or their outlandishly oversized cookies. But there they were on my little phone: enormous disks of perfectly formed cookie that appeared to be about the size of the peanut's head. Instagram posts showed towers of multihued varietals, some the telltale color of red velvet, others that were ambiguous shades of brown. They all looked soft but crunchy, easily a half-inch thick. They all looked incredible. It wasn't enough to just admire them from afar. Their massive, crackling edges and tender middles were too good to pass up. One gray day in December, I strapped the peanut snuggly to my chest and made my maiden voyage to the closet-sized subterranean bakery in Chelsea.

City Cakes opened as a custom cake business in 2008—just a few months before I left for Paris, which made me feel ever so slightly better about having been previously oblivious to it. Run by two chefs, Benny Rivera, the "artistic" one, and Marc Coolrecht, the "business" one, they were cruising right along for a couple years, churning out cakes in the shapes of guitars, chessboards, sailboats, and other fanciful commissions, in flavors like strawberry champagne, cinnamon swirl, and Caribbean brandy. In order to get more customers familiar with their cakes without having to order a custom creation, Benny and Marc decided to open a retail front.

To begin, they offered cupcakes in their various flavors— red velvet, double chocolate, precious yellow cake—and threw in four kinds of cookies to round out their offering: chocolate chip, triple chocolate spice, oatmeal raisin, and peanut butter with Reese's Pieces. While the cake business continued to thrive with customers like Jennifer Lopez and Fergie placing custom orders, and their masterful work being showcased everywhere from *The Rachel Ray Show* to *InStyle* magazine, their cookies quickly became fan favorites— especially once a third team member, Sarah Pleitez, came aboard and brought even more flavors.

Sarah joined City Cakes in 2011 as an intern and quickly demonstrated a knack for creating recipes, despite not having a sweet tooth. "I didn't even know what Reese's Pieces were when I started," she confesses. This is something I do not understand—how could anyone not intimately know the whole Reese's repertoire?—but it's proven to be a nonissue. Sarah's personal ambition and devotion to recipe development drove her to doubling City Cakes' cookie roster without a dud yet.

Sarah's first introduction was the signature sugardoodle. Big, billowy, and buttery, sparkling with a generous coating of sugar crystals and cinnamon, it has the perfect savory-sweet balance that comes from creamed butter and sugar. When she created it, the bakery's cookie menu was dominated by chocolaty options. She was looking to add something with a different flavor profile. Then, for the 2013 holiday season, she was playing with recipe ideas that would evoke nostalgia and home baking and struck upon the ginger spice cookie, a soft, sweet molasses number with the bite of ginger, cinnamon, and nutmeg. It was so popular it stuck around beyond the holidays and became a year-round best seller. Then came the killer red velvet. Rich from cocoa, savory from a cream cheese center, and crunchy from its sugar-dusted top, it gives red velvet lovers a whole new creation to die for.

Sarah, Benny, and the City Cakes crew is constantly working with trends and seasonal inspirations and soliciting customer feedback and suggestions to come up with new flavors. But it's "an intense production," Sarah points out of the cookies they offer. "We can only have so many." The bakery's diminutive size limits their ability to experiment too much. Their custom cakes remain the driving force of their business and the cookie mania has to be capped at some point.

When I went for the first time, I figured it wasn't worth the hike from Brooklyn to just get one cookie. So I got three: the triple chocolate spice, killer red velvet, and sugardoodle. The bakery, a no-frills spot at the bottom of a rickety staircase on Eighteenth Street, packaged them in a box as if I were bringing them to a ladies' tea. Instead, I devoured what amounted to a pound and a half of fresh baked goods before I even made it back to Brooklyn.

Each flavor was familiar but unique and had a whole lot going for it: the force of spices that erupted from the triple chocolate spice, the savory cream cheese center of the red velvet, and, my favorite, the billowy, sweet, touched-with-cinnamon sugardoodle. They were creative but not outrageous—traditional with a twist, if you will. Every bite had a satisfying crunch that gave way to a soft, just barely warm center. The ingredients and dough were balanced to decadent perfection, not overly sweet, not overdone, just a titch undercooked. With each one, I found myself committing to a new obsession.

Meanwhile, the peanut remained asleep in her carrier, having fed before we left the apartment and been lulled to sleep by the train's rhythmic motion. We were one bloated belly pressed to another, and she was oblivious to the soft rain of crumbs that fell all around her and her mama's orgasmic delight. And neither was Andrew any the wiser that his wife was loose in the city, flaunting a dysfunctional relationship—with cookies.

So during those long days, did I miss work? Crave adult conversation? Want intellectual stimulation? Hell no. I was happy to spend my maternity leave watching *Footloose* on cable, eating my loot from the great outdoors, and cuddling with the peanut on the couch while the rest of the world schlepped to the subway in the snow.

Think about it: for four months, I wore no makeup. I didn't do my hair. I rotated between two outfits. I could eat what I wanted, when and where I wanted. I didn't have to set the alarm for work or waste even one second diddling over what to wear. None of it mattered. It was women's liberation of a whole new kind. When else would I ever have an excuse to live like that?

My maternity leave marched on through the dead of winter, and it was a brutal one at that. Through the holidays and January, it was cold and blustery, with one snowstorm after another. But what did I care? There were days when I never even got out of my pajamas. Days that the longest trip I took was from the couch to the refrigerator. Days when I did my breastfeeding and laundry and crossword puzzles while binging on *Girlfriends' Guide to Divorce, Love It or List It,* and bad eighties movies while the peanut napped on my shoulder, snuggled into that heavenly nook. It was wonderful to give my brain a rest. It occurred to me this was the first time in two and a half decades, since my first job whipping up Oreo Blizzards at Dairy Queen, that I allowed myself to do nothing—though Andrew kindly reminded me that keeping the peanut alive every day was hardly "doing nothing." Admittedly, it was a big job—the biggest and most important of my life—and when it wasn't frustrating the hell out of me or scaring me to death, it was heaven. I was so content being warm and happy inside with our new baby girl, immune to the elements and the rest of the world outside.

I was warm and happy for the other obvious reason: it was the second time in just a couple of years that I was head over heels in love.

Falling in love with Andrew had been slow and steady.

Wave after wave, getting bigger, deeper, and more profound until I was pulled under. With the peanut, it was an intense storm: lightning bolts; pounding elements; a fierce, overwhelming drive that scared me. I loved her until it hurt and I cried.

Week by week, I watched in amazement as she developed before me. Her belly ballooned and her legs formed delicious rolls. She started smiling and cooing. Soon, her eyes would light up in recognition of my or Andrew's face. I loved kissing her fuzzy, little head and stroking her insanely soft cheeks. Squeezing her thighs and tickling her knees. The peanut would lie on her activity mat and was soon reaching for the dangling apples and parrots above, or learning how to navigate the white bear rattle with her tiny matchstick fingers. I'd watch as her lips puckered in concentration and her legs kicked when she got excited. Every day, she seemed to be learning new tricks. As she did, we both became more confident—her in this big, new world and me in this big, new role. While I still obsessed over how many ounces of breast milk she consumed a day and diligently tracked how many hours she'd sleep at night in one go, at least I was no longer hallucinating or flailing. I came to understand that even if I felt clueless, I could trust that I would figure things out. I started relaxing and having more fun. I'd cranked up the Yeah Yeah Yeahs, dancing with the peanut held tightly in my arms, my emotions swinging with the beat, until suddenly my throat ached and I was swallowing back tears as I sang with the heavenly Karen O:

Flow sweetly, hang heavy
You suddenly complete me
You suddenly complete me

There was no going back. This little girl now owned my heart.

Those were my good, albeit emotional, days. There were plenty of rough ones too.

Despite alternately reveling in my private feminist movement and acting like a moony teenager, parenthood was an enormous adjustment. Forty-plus years of independence and suddenly I was a slave to a baby. Yes, I got in crossword puzzles and became familiar with Instagram and ate with force and glee, but my life was no longer my own. As much time as I had, it was parsed into these impossibly distracted, abbreviated spurts where I had to be able to drop everything at a given moment to tend to the peanut. I couldn't trot off to the gym or a movie, lose myself in a book, or even compose a coherent thought. I was cut off from friends, current events, and culture. And there was the added layer of not feeling like a writer.

Even though I had this monumental new dimension to

my life—wife and mother—it felt belittling to have nothing to do with writerly pursuits. There was no trolling New York's restaurants and bakeries in the name of good reportage. No scheming to go to Sicily to write about the most luxurious spa treatments. No satisfying deliveries of the Sunday paper to see my byline. I had consciously pulled back from my freelance pursuits, but now I was so removed from this former life that I sort of even missed the rejection of pitching an article.

Writing had become such a big part of my identity over the years. And yet there I was, not writing one lick of anything. Even more disconcerting, I didn't *want* to. My ambition had vanished. I was suddenly taking pride in keeping up on the laundry, not New York's restaurant scene. Did that mean I was no longer a writer? Would I be able to still land assignments if and when the urge to pitch struck again? I did my best to shove aside the fears that more than two decades of career building was for naught if I didn't publish something, like, soon.

Of course it's when you're finally feeling competent, like you have a clue as to how to provide for your baby and are in a groove with their rhythms and needs, that you're expected to go back to work. And God bless America, *one of four countries in the world* without paid parental leave laws. Saudi Arabia offers paid parental leave. China, Mongolia, and Haiti offer paid parental leave. African nations like Togo and Zimbabwe pay 100 percent of a woman's earnings for fourteen weeks when they have a child. America offers nothing. So when our dear politicians are espousing family values, all they really care about is having women shut up and stay at home.

Fortunately, a lot of companies, particularly in the tech sector, are creating their own generous policies. But the best our government has done is pass the 1993 Family and Medical Leave Act (FMLA), which guarantees your job if you take unpaid leave for up to twelve weeks for a family or medical reason. It's something. But if you've ever had, held, or seen a twelve-week-old baby, you know how crazy it is to imagine that child being ready part with its mother. A twelve-week-old baby is a teeny, helpless thing. It's not healthy, it's not right, for the mother to go back to work so soon after childbirth.

I received partial pay from my company for those twelve weeks protected by the FMLA, and I took another four weeks of unpaid time off so I could be with the peanut a wee bit longer. The last month proved to be so important, as it was the first time I had enough wherewithal to actually look ahead instead of drowning in the moment. I could see all the things besides breastfeeding and laundry that needed to be done. I had to figure out how to pump so I could create a stockpile of breast milk in the freezer, for when I was no longer at home to feed the peanut. I had to start engaging

with the real world again, not just Instagram and HGTV. I
had to get back into a professional mindset and wardrobe. I
had to warm up to the idea of socializing on a daily basis. I
had to get a haircut. And most importantly, Andrew and I
had to find a nanny, someone whom we did not yet know
and but would trust our baby's life with.

This process was another bizarrely foreign one to us. We
found about a half dozen viable candidates by soliciting
referrals from other parents on the Internet. Then we invited
these women into our home, analyzed how fresh their clothes
appeared, if they washed their hands immediately upon enter-
ing (I was still so anxious about someone from the outside
coming in and infecting the peanut's pristine system with
germs), and if they could look me in the eye and respond
articulately to my barrage of carefully researched questions. I
scrutinized how they interacted with the peanut and, indeed,
whether they did, as some didn't even acknowledge her. Most
of all, I was checking for that gut feeling. I wanted to know
in my heart, head, and bones that our nanny was going to be
the best choice for the peanut.

Such were my anxious thoughts as the last weeks of maternity leave ticked by. With the end looming before me, at least
I was figuring this stuff out. I had conquered the breast pump
and was slowly building a stash of breast milk in the freezer. I
had even forced myself to go out to lunch one day so I could
face the fear of breastfeeding for the first time in public. I

had done some online shopping and could envision myself resuming professional duties at the office. And after several weeks of searching, interviewing, and deliberating, we found our nanny. I first left the peanut with her for two hours, then four, then six, getting used to what it felt like to entrust our baby girl with another caregiver. I was doing everything my type-A brain could think of to get ready to go to work again, and according to my checklist, I was ready. But apparently my psyche never got the memo.

Of Paris, I used to say I experienced the highest highs and lowest lows of my life. I now realized being a new mom was ten times as intense. It was such incredible joy and love, mixed with some of the deepest challenges and darkest moments. In hindsight, it's not surprising that two weeks before I was to return to work, I lost it. After months of devoting myself so wholly to doing the best I could with the peanut and semis-uccessfully navigating the mix of emotions that went with it, something snapped inside of me.

It started as just another ordinary-extraordinary day. Andrew was at work and had dinner plans in the evening, so he'd be gone later than usual. The peanut and I enjoyed our hours together, me doing laundry and breastfeeding, her doing tummy time and eating. Every so often, I felt a wave of emotion that was a little sharper and more overwhelming than usual. At one point, as I gently lowered the peanut onto her activity mat on the floor, I dropped her. She was only about four inches off the ground, but her startled cries and the thud of her hitting tore through my chest. I was a wreck. I felt incompetent. I kept willing the tears to go away, but as day turned to evening, I couldn't contain them anymore. They were no longer waves of emotions; they were tsunamis. By the time I tried to read her *On the Night You Were Born*, one of the dozens of belovedly sappy baby books in regular rotation at bedtime, I started crying—really crying. Heaving sobs that I couldn't stop. I couldn't get the words of the book out. I couldn't see through my tears. I thought was going crazy.

The reality was, all those weeks of being at home with no outside obligations, just me and my girl cuddled on the couch, were soon to be—*poof*—over. Four glorious months of being with that little creature twenty-four-seven, her protector and provider; just the two of us, figuring things out together, being so dependent on one another—they were never to be again. It had been such a precious experience and, I realized, I just didn't want maternity leave to be over. As cut off from the world as I'd been, as physically and culturally stunted as I was, as depleting as the daily tasks could be, that time with the peanut had been nothing short of magic. I had spent more consistent time with her than anyone in my life. We'd never have that much uninterrupted time together again. She would never be that little again. It slayed me that it would be no more.

When Andrew came home, I clung to him in the entryway, trying to explain what was wrong with me. But I couldn't. I couldn't articulate my feelings. All I could really express was that I was so *sad*. I was also trying to reassure him that, even though I could barely speak because I was crying so hard, everything was okay, with both the peanut and me.

Because I knew that it was. I knew maternity leave was precious in part because it was finite. If I had been going to lose my autonomy and ambition completely, if I had had no creative or professional outlet to eventually look forward to, I probably would have gone batty. And while my love for the peanut was overwhelming, it wasn't going anywhere. I knew it would only grow as she grew bigger, day by day, and become just as dependent on the nanny as me and Andrew. But for now, she was soundly sleeping in her crib and I just had to quell this cocktail of anxiety, fear, sorrow, and devotion. I knew these things, but what I felt that night was so different. Andrew held me until I stopped crying and finally drifted off to sleep.

After that small taste of postpartum depression, which I realized I was so lucky not to have suffered from, I started feeling like I could do it. I could let go of the beautiful experience it had been, knowing I would carry it in my heart forever. Knowing there were many new beginnings for me and the peanut in the years ahead and it would be ever more beautiful. For now, it was time to return to work. To reunite with my colleagues. To welcome a new routine and use those rusty creative parts of my brain again. And, who knew? Maybe I'd even get back to writing.

THE BEST CHOCOLATE CHIP COOKIES IN TOWN

Where to begin. How to evaluate. Why do we have to choose just one? There are so many amazing cookies in this big, beautiful city and the task of choosing the best is too difficult. To cap the madness, let's just talk about chocolate chip cookies.

Ever since my friend Julie introduced me to the six-ounce-dense and chocolaty cookies at Levain Bakery on the Upper West Side, they have been my favorite. Along with melty semisweet chips, they're packed with walnuts and have a thickly undercooked, cakey texture that sends my heart soaring.

City Bakery in the Flatiron District makes chocolate chip cookies that are thin and flat, the antithesis of Levain's. Their addictive crunchy texture is slick with butter, gritty from sugar, and studded with big hunks of chocolate. Naughty.

Just one look, and you know Smile to Go in SoHo has the salty-sweet technique down to perfection. Each cookie's surface features four to six perfectly circular disks of chocolate that are little magnets for flaked sea salt, giving each bite a one-two punch.

Maman came to town when I was on maternity leave and quickly became another obsession. This

Franco-American bakery, with locations in SoHo, Tribeca, and Greenpoint, layers their chocolate chip cookie with macadamia nuts, almonds, and walnuts, and sometimes pretzels, because why not?

In addition to his own chunks of rich, 60 percent dark chocolate, the secret weapon to French chocolatier Jacques Torres's cookies is a warming apparatus. When you get a cookie at one of his chocolate shops, you can be assured that your treat will be warm, gooey, and leave streaks of chocolate on your greedy little fingers.

CHAPTER 13

Afternoon Delights

Day by day, month by month, normalcy was restored. *Is* restored. My new life of sleep deprivation, emotional turbulence, and mad love is the new reality. As they say, having a kid changes everything.

I ended up going back to work a week before my maternity leave ended. The agency was in a new business pitch for a legendary skin cream that costs as much as a week's worth of groceries, and the managing director called to see if I could help out. I reluctantly agreed, and it set the tone for my first month back at the office. For once that first pitch was over, there was another. And then another. Between the intensity and pace of work, the rude reintroduction to commuting, and dealing emotionally with suddenly being separated from the peanut, it nearly did me in.

New business pitches are notoriously manic, called only

somewhat facetiously "pitch theater." You're tasked with coming up with amazing work in a short amount of time. Not just smart, creative ideas, but ones that are going to be "groundbreaking" and "revolutionary." Ones that will "go viral" and "disrupt the status quo." They obviously need to be "out of the box" and "break through the clutter." In other words, the client expectations and internal scrutiny are absurd. We'd be in meetings every evening at six o'clock, reviewing the day's work. I wanted to sound and appear like a competent, committed creative leader, but inside I was screaming: *Who cares about this cream's magic ingredient? Why are we quibbling about "radiant" versus "luminous" when exactly .005 percent of the population will ever read the copy? Don't you guys realize: the peanut is hungry?!* Though I was fortunate enough to work with enlightened people who intuited my distress and told me to go as the minute hand crept farther past the hour, it was stressful to say the least. As badly as I wanted to get home, I felt like a slacker leaving those meetings night after night.

Even after that initial pitch phase, I struggled to put on a brave face and appear unfazed by the internal chaos of my mind. I literally ran to and from the subway every day—which wasn't a bad thing, since I hadn't worked out in five months, but it wasn't exactly a healthy emotional place. I always felt behind. Always pulled between two places. As anxious as I was about how the peanut was doing without me, I worried about how I was doing at my job. Was everyone taking me seriously? Had I lost my touch? *Was I good enough?*

Adding to the stress was my new responsibility at work: pumping. I really believed the peanut would be stronger, healthier, and better for life if she had only breast milk in her pristine little system for the first six months (*who you calling a Teat Nazi?*). And she was a voracious eater. My stockpile of breast milk in the freezer was quickly dwindling. So two or three times a day, I'd scamper off to an oversized closet that HR had designated as a pump room, strip from the waist up, and hook up these god-awful contraptions to my breasts, flipping the switch of a compact motorized pump that would milk me for all I was worth. If my colleagues were onto why I mysteriously disappeared for chunks of time throughout the day, they at least pretended not to be, sparing me a tiny shred of dignity.

Over time—albeit a long time—it got better. Or rather I just got better with the idea of being a working mom, trying to reconcile having both a demanding career and a baby— and, not for nothing, a new and fabulous husband. It was at least a year before I didn't have a mini-panic-attack rushing home in order to feed the peanut, relishing the feel of her soft, downy hair beneath my chin, and spend a little time with her before she went to sleep. Even now, I feel self-conscious when I pack up my bag to go home at six o'clock. I'm almost always the first one to leave the office—that is, if I'm not working late, which is unfortunately a regular occurrence. That's advertising. That's today's workplace. We live in an age where we're expected to work like we're not raising kids and to raise kids like we're not also working. And I, along with millions of other women like me, have learned to just deal with it.

Just as I've had to adapt to a new life-work balance, our social life has been an adjustment. It can be cleanly divided into BP and AP (Before the Peanut and After the Peanut).

BP, for example, a good birthday party was when we got liquored up and sweaty on some crowded downtown dance floor, unironically dancing with about a dozen friends to what millennials consider old-school music.

AP, a good birthday party includes listening to some hippie chick strum her guitar to a room full of one- and two-year-olds, singing about buses and animals at the zoo, instead of assholes who broke her heart, leaving us adults hands free long enough to scarf down as much pizza and wine as we possibly can before our children spiral out of control and start climbing all over us again.

BP, Andrew and I indulged our wanderlust, relished spontaneity, and overspent abroad. We scouted out romantic inns and stayed at cool boutique hotels. We made love often and ate dinner late at night.

AP, we look for hotels—or hospitable friends—with rooms

big and luxurious enough to accommodate the three of us and make it worth schlepping a trunk full of baby gear, but not so posh that we're terrified of disrupting anyone's peace, pissing anyone off, or ruining that beautiful beige bedspread with an accidental spill of pureed purple carrots.

BP, we had our urban treks and midday cocktails on the weekends.

AP, we spend weekends lounging on the living room floor, doing puzzles, building block towers, and having tea parties.

BP, date night might have involved the symphony, dinner at a buzzy restaurant, and a nightcap at a rooftop bar.

AP, staying in is the new going out. Once the peanut is down for the night, we bust out our pint of Ample Hills, pour two tumblers of Armagnac, and settle in for a binge-worthy series like *The Americans, Veep, Bloodline,* or *Louie.* A couple of hours later, tired and sated, we head to bed already anticipating our inevitable crack-of-dawn wake-up call.

BP, we duked it out for highly prized reservations and felt proud of the bragging rights that came with dining at the city's most au courant restaurants.

AP, we go for the early bird special: seated at six, done eating by eight, home in bed by ten.

But it turns out, hitting restaurants at such an un-chic hour, without battling those pesky thirtysomething, restaurant-obsessed urbanites for a table, and getting unceremoniously rushed by managers and servers who want to turn tables, is actually a lovely way to enjoy each other's company along with a good meal. It turns out, getting squeezed from the conventionally cool territories we used to inhabit has been just fine for us—more than fine. Now that everything has been turned upside down and fundamentally rewritten, a big night out for us is a day out.

While we still had a dearth of babysitters to rely on in the evenings, we now knew our nanny was one hundred percent competent. If we could leave the peanut with her for ten hours a day to go to work, why not use that time and freedom and go out and play? As yet another birthday rolled around (how was I turning forty-three already?!), we gave it a whirl.

Our nanny arrived like any other morning, relieving us at the normal hour. But that day was like a get-out-of-jail-free card. We left the apartment and were midstream all the commuters—that we weren't also trudging off to the office was the first of many highs that day. We stopped at Joyce Bakery, tucked a couple spinach-and-cheese croissants inside my bag, and then hopped on the train to the Union Square Regal cinema for a 10:00 a.m. matinee. A movie, first thing in the morning! It was so indulgent, just us and a handful of retirees, enjoying a big Hollywood production—our first in over a year. It was like when I first moved to the city and every little outing filled me with excitement, everything felt new and special. I settled into my chair that morning, enjoyed the bombardment of crazy trailers before the movie along with my contraband croissant, and looked forward to what was next: cocktails and lunch at Gramercy Tavern, one of our all-time favorite restaurants.

When Danny Meyer opened Gramercy Tavern in 1994 with Tom Colicchio (of Bravo's *Top Chef* fame), he was going for the vibe of "an animated community hall," as he wrote in the restaurant's official cookbook. He envisioned it as a love child of his first restaurant, Union Square Café, and Taillevent, the acclaimed three-Michelin-star restaurant in Paris. He wanted elegance without the stuffiness, exquisite service that was also down-to-earth. A welcoming place for customers to gather, drink, and enjoy the best seasonal food available. And that's exactly what it is. Gramercy's back dining room is hushed and ever more formal; the tavern up front is walk-in only and always packed with people who couldn't be happier to be enveloped in the friendly atmosphere, with the prospect of excellent drinks and dishes on the horizon.

"There's nothing better than Gramercy in November" is what Chef Michael Anthony remembers always hearing when he took over the kitchen from Colicchio in 2006. And it's true. The golden colors of the towering floral arrangements and baskets of gourds that sit on the restaurant's antique pie chests and cabinets, picking up the bold hues from the twenty-panel Robert Kushner mural that hangs over the bar, create an enveloping autumnal feeling. But Michael wanted to become everyone's favorite restaurant in *every* season.

Michael, who had trained and cooked in Tokyo and Paris, and was working at Chef Daniel Boulud's renowned restaurant Daniel before Gramercy, had been instilled with the philosophy that if consistency is your goal, you will only reach mediocrity. Which means you *have to* change every day. You must listen attentively to your team; be partners with your food purveyors, nurturing a deeper dialogue about how they're growing their food; and push every employee to keep evolving and inventing. There is no settling. You recreate the identity of the restaurant over and over again. This all seems a bit counterintuitive because Gramercy Tavern itself is a classic. People love the restaurant for the very reason that it is tried, true, and familiar. It's a place that preserves the tradition around eating. And somehow Michael has managed to protect the integrity of the restaurant while refusing to cook the same things over and over.

"There are no real signature dishes on the menu," he states emphatically. Gramercy may rotate things that were created years ago, but they're revisited at different times, in different seasons, evolving with ingredients and inspiration that come from the team in the kitchen. To support the needs of this ever-changing credo, Michael created several in-house programs at Gramercy, including a pasta program.

It was, not surprisingly, a pasta that caught my and Andrew's attention on a BP night at the bar. What was surprising was that it was mushroom lasagna, as I'm not a big mushroom fan. But it sounded so amazing: layers of mascarpone, mushrooms, and béchamel, accented with thyme. "It's an exercise in aesthetics more than the recipe," the chef claims of the dish. He created it in the winter of 2007/08 in collaboration with his then-sous-chef Nick Anderer, who has since gone onto Maialino and Marta, two other Danny Meyer restaurants. The flat sheaves of house-made pasta are cut by hand and layered with the cheese and mushrooms, creating a rich, earthy, and divine flavor. What's more, the texture is pitch-perfect. The unctuousness of the filling contrasts with the crispy, charred pasta that gets singed and smoky in the eight-hundred-degree oven. "It's a true iconic American dish," Michael agrees.

That day when we went to Gramercy for my birthday, the menu didn't have lasagna on it. And so, appropriately AP, we moved on to a new favorite: the flatbread appetizer.

The flatbread arrived on the restaurant's menu in a totally different fashion than the lasagna. Whereas Michael specifically developed the pasta program to make the noodles in-house for dishes like the lasagna, the flatbread was inspired from an outside source. "I fell in love with a North African flatbread," he says of the *m'smen* baked at Hot Bread Kitchen, a thriving bakery incubator in East Harlem. "It lit our imaginations up." The savory, hand-stretched bread is like a blank canvas, one that Michael and his kitchen crew top in countless ways from clam, celery root, and *salsa verde* to corn, green tomatoes, and lamb sausage to pickled peppers and mushrooms. "I love that it's shareable and just about as informal as you can imagine," the chef says.

Andrew and I shared everything that day, as we always do, including the chocolate pudding cake that the bartender presented with a candle because she overheard us talking about my birthday. That's the kind of restaurant it is. That is why it is so beloved by not just me and Andrew, but also the entire city. As Michael says, "Ten years after working at Gramercy Tavern, people are more in love with that restaurant than ever before."

For all of my bellyaching about being old, afraid, out of touch, chronically tired, and culturally stunted, there is so much to love about this phase of my life—my act two. I'd be lying if I said I didn't have pangs of missing my earlier carefree adventures, both solo and with Andrew. But there are new joys: retrieving the peanut from her crib in the morning and relishing how happy she is to see me in that moment as I scoop her in my arms. Hearing her laugh, a true, unselfconscious belly laugh. And there is the simple pleasure of loving someone so deeply and completely.

The love runs just as deep with Andrew. He has proven to be everything I could want: affectionate, fun, sincere, devoted, and a true partner when it comes to dull tasks such as changing diapers and creating savings plans. I think he's even more handsome today than when we met at Park Bar five years ago, and he still surprises me with his knowledge, sensitivity, compassion, and lust for life. The two of us still laugh about the fact that we met online and still have a great time just parking it on the couch with Netflix and a pint of Ample Hills or, on special occasions, Levain cookies.

And then there is Brooklyn. Each passing month accumulated into years, I begin to feel more at home. It's neither the idealized bohemian utopia nor the suburban trap I believed it to be at earlier points on the journey. I see it now in a new and fairer light. I know it's perfect for where I am in my life. We spend summer evenings picnicking in Prospect Park, Andrew and I sipping wine while the peanut runs around the great lawn, surrounded by other families of all different nationalities and backgrounds. We can go to a bar with the peanut and no one bats an eye—because there are always at least a few other couples with babies there. Restaurants are tolerant of a little one sitting in my lap, spilling crumbs all over the floor (though, for the record, I always pick that mess up before we leave, amen). And there are strollers absolutely everywhere.

I stand by the idea that Andrew and I would have had a wonderful, fulfilling life if it were just the two of us. And yet, now that the peanut is here, I can't imagine it any other way. After years of alternately priding myself on being single and independent and wondering if and when I would ever fall in love again and have a baby; after living a fantasy, achieving my dream, and not knowing where to go from there, I finally found my way home. As foreign as it all seemed at the beginning, this is it. Exactly the life I'm meant to be living.

ALL ABOUT — THE — HOSPITALITY

Danny Meyer has based his entire career on making his employees, customers, and business partners feel happy and well taken care of— which all comes through in the experience of dining at his restaurants. Each one of them is delicious and memorable. Here is a select list of his establishments, in order of ascending fanciness.

Shake Shack—The now multinational, publically traded fast-food chain was inspired by the roadside burger stands from Danny's youth in the Midwest and serves burgers, dogs, and concretes—frozen custard blended with mix-ins, including Mast Brothers chocolate and Four & Twenty Blackbirds pie, depending on the location.

Blue Smoke—Another nod to Danny's upbringing in the Midwest, this Murray Hill barbecue joint features all manner of pit from chargrilled oysters to fried chicken to seven-pepper brisket, along with a jazz club in the basement.

Maialino—This warm and rustic Roman-style trattoria with its garganelli and braised rabbit and suckling pig with rosemary potatoes is the antidote to the fancypants Gramercy Park Hotel, in which it resides.

Untitled—When the Whitney Museum moved from the Upper East Side to the Meatpacking District, the in-house coffee shop was reincarnated as a fine dining restaurant, with none other than Chef Michael Anthony running the kitchen, serving the likes of duck liver paté, parsnip and potato chowder, and a triple chocolate chunk cookie served with a shot of milk.

Union Square Café—As of late 2016, this New York classic has a new home on Park Avenue South. But it has the same style, soul, and classic menu—Anson Mills polenta, ricotta gnocchi, new york strip steak—as it first did when Danny opened the restaurant back in 1985.

The Modern—Overlooking the Miró, Matisse, and Picasso sculptures in MoMA's Sculpture Garden, the dishes here are appropriately refined and artistic. Think cauliflower roasted in crab butter, sautéed foie gras, and crispy Long Island duck.

List of Eateries

Brooklyn

al di la Trattoria
248 Fifth Avenue (Park Slope)
aldilatrattoria.com

Ample Hills
623 Vanderbilt Avenue
   (Prospect Heights)
305 Nevins Street (Gowanus)
amplehills.com

Baked
359 Van Brunt Street (Red Hook)
bakednyc.com

Blue Sky Bakery
53 Fifth Avenue (Park Slope)
blueskybakery.org

Buttermilk Channel
524 Court Street (Carroll Gardens)
buttermilkchannelnyc.com

Cacao Prieto
218 Conover Street
   (Red Hook)
cacaoprieto.com

Dough
448 Lafayette Aveneue (Bed-Stuy)
doughdoughnuts.com

Eric Kayser
57 Court Street
   (Brooklyn Heights)
maison-kayser-usa.com

The Farm on Adderly

1108 Cortelyou Road
(Ditmas Park)
thefarmonadderley.com

Fort Defiance

365 Van Brunt Street
(Red Hook)
fortdefiancebrooklyn.com

Four & Twenty Blackbirds

439 Third Avenue
(Gowanus)
birdsblack.com

Frankies 457 Spuntino

457 Court Street
(Carroll Gardens)
frankiesspuntino.com

Franny's

348 Flatbush Avenue
(Park Slope)
frannysbrooklyn.com

The Good Fork

391 Van Brunt Street
(Red Hook)
goodfork.com

Henry Public

329 Henry Street (Cobble Hill)
henrypublic.com

Home/Made

293 Van Brunt Street (Red Hook)
homemadebklyn.com

Jack the Horse Tavern

66 Hicks Street
(Brooklyn Heights)
jackthehorse.com

Jacques Torres

66 Water Street (Dumbo)
mrchocolate.com

James

605 Carlton Avenue
(Prospect Heights)
jamesrestaurantny.com

Lavender Lake

383 Carroll Street
(Gowanus)
lavendarlake.com

Locanda Vini e Olii

129 Gates Avenue (Clinton Hill)
locandany.com

Maman
80 Kent Street (Greenpoint)
mamannyc.com

Mast Brothers Factory
111 North Third Street
   (Williamsburg)
mastbrothers.com

Milk Bar
360 Smith Street
   (Carroll Gardens)
382 Metropolitan Avenue
   (Williamsburg)
milkbarstore.com

Oddfellows Ice Cream Co.
175 Kent Avenue (Williamsburg)
oddfellowsnyc.com

Rucola
190 Dean Street (Boerum Hill)
rucolabrooklyn.com

Sharlene's
353 Flatbush Avenue
   (Prospect Heights)
718.618.0282

Speedy Romeo
376 Classon Avenue
   (Clinton Hill)
speedyromeo.com

Steve's Authentic Key Lime Pie
185 Van Dyke Street
   (Red Hook)
718.858.5333

Sugar Shop
254 Baltic Street (Cobble Hill)
sugarshopbrooklyn.com

Vinegar Hill House
72 Hudson Avenue (Dumbo)
vinegarhillhouse.com

Manhattan

Ample Hills
Inside Gotham West Market
  (Midtown West)
600 Eleventh Avenue

At Bubby's High Line
73 Gansevoort Street
  (Meatpacking)
amplehills.com

Arturo's
106 West Houston Street
  (Greenwich Village)
212.677.3820

Barbuto
775 Washington Street
  (West Village)
barbutonyc.com

Bemelmans Bar at The Carlyle
25 East Seventy-Sixth Street
  (Upper East Side)
212.744.1600

Big Gay Ice Cream
125 East Seventh Street
  (East Village)
61 Grove Street (West Village)
biggayicecream.com

Billy's Bakery
184 Ninth Avenue (Chelsea)
75 Franklin Street (Tribeca)
billys-bakery.myshopify.com

Birdbath Bakery
160 Prince Street (SoHo)
45 Spring Street (Nolita)
140 East Forty-Fifth Street
  (Midtown)
2244 Broadway (Upper West Side)

Blue Hill
75 Washington Place
  (Greenwich Village)
bluehillfarm.com

Blue Smoke
116 East Twenty-Seventh Street
  (Gramercy)
255 Vesey Street (Battery Park)
bluesmoke.com

Bosie Tea Parlor
10 Morton Street (West Village)
bosieteaparlor.com

Butter Lane
123 East Seventh Street
   (East Village)
butterlane.com

Buvette
42 Grove Street (West Village)
buvette.com

City Bakery
3 West Eighteenth Street
   (Flatiron)
thecitybakery.com

City Cakes
251 West Eighteenth Street
   (Chelsea)
citycakes.com

The Crosby Bar at the Crosby Street Hotel
79 Crosby Street (SoHo)
212.226.6400

DBGB
299 Bowery (Bowery)
dbgb.com/nyc

Dessert Club, ChikaLicious
204 East Tenth Street
   (East Village)
dessertclubnyc.com

Dominique Ansel
189 Spring Street (SoHo)
dominiqueansel.com

Dough
14 West Nineteenth Street
   (Flatiron)
doughdoughnuts.com

Eleven Madison Park
11 Madison Avenue
   (Madison Park)
elevenmadisonpark.com

Eric Kayser
355 Greenwich Street (Tribeca)
326 Bleecker Street (West Village)
841 Broadway (Union Square)
921 Broadway (Flatiron)
8 West Fortieth Street (Midtown)
1800 Broadway (Upper West Side)
2161 Broadway (Upper West Side)
1294 Third Avenue (Upper East Side)
1535 Third Avenue (Upper East Side)
maison-kayser-usa.com

Gramercy Tavern
42 East Twentieth Street
  (Gramery)
gramercytavern.com

The Half King
505 West Twenty-Third Street
  (Chelsea)
thehalfking.com

Il Buco
47 Bond Street (NoHo)
ilbuco.com

Il Buco Alimentari
e Vineria
53 Great Jones Street
  (NoHo)
ilbucovineria.com

Il Cantinori
32 East Tenth Street
  (Greenwich Village)
incantinori.com

Ice & Vice
221 East Broadway
  (Lower East Side)
iceandvice.com

Jacques Torres
350 Hudson Street (SoHo)
285 Amsterdam Avenue
  (Upper West Side)
30 Rockefeller Plaza
  (Midtown)
110 East Fifty-Seventh Street
  (Midtown)
327 Lafayette Street (NoHo)
mrchocolate.com

The King Cole Bar
at the St. Regis
2 East Fifty-Fifth Street
  (Midtown)
stregisnewyork.com

Ladurée
864 Madison Avenue
  (Upper East Side)
398 West Broadway (SoHo)
laduree.com

Levain Bakery
167 West Seventy-Fourth Street
  (Upper West Side)
2167 Frederick Douglass
  Boulevard (Harlem)
levainbakery.com

The Lobby Lounge at
the Mandarin Oriental
80 Columbus Circle
   (Upper West Side)
212.805.8800

Maialino in the
Gramercy Hotel
2 Lexington Avenue
   (Gramercy)
maialinonyc.com

Maman
239 Centre Street (SoHo)
211 West Broadway (Tribeca)
mamannyc.com

Milk Bar
251 East Thirteenth Street
   (East Village)
15 West Fifty-Sixth Street
   (Midtown)
561 Broadway
   (Upper West Side)
220 Eighth Avenue
   (Chelsea)
246 Mott Street
   (Nolita)
74 Christopher Street
   (West Village)
milkbarstore.com

Minetta Tavern
113 Macdougal Street
   (Greenwich Village)
minettatavernny.com

The Modern at the
Museum of Modern Art
9 West Fifty-Third Street
   (Midtown)
themodernnyc.com

Morgenstern's Finest
Ice Cream
2 Rivington Street
   (Bowery)
morgensternsnyc.com

The Musket Room
265 Elizabeth Street
   (Nolita)
musketroom.com

OddFellows Ice Cream Co.
75 East Fourth Street
   (East Village)
oddfellowsnyc.com

Park Bar
15 East Fifteenth Street
   (Union Square)
parkbarnyc.com

Piora
430 Hudson Street
    (West Village)
pioranyc.com

Rebelle
218 Bowery (Bowery)
rebellenyc.com

Salon de Ning
at the Peninsula
700 Fifth Avenue (Midtown)
212.956.2888

The Smile to Go
22 Howard Street (SoHo)
thesmilenyc.com

Sugar Sweet Sunshine
128 Rivington Street
    (Lower East Side)
sugarsweetsunshine.com

Sweet Revenge
62 Carmine Street
    (West Village)
sweetrevengenyc.com

Tom & Jerry's
288 Elizabeth Street
    (NoHo)
212.260.5045

Terroir
24 Harrison Street
    (Tribeca)
wineisterrior.com

Union Square Café
101 East Nineteenth Street
    (Union Square)
unionsquarecafe.com

Untitled at the Whitney
99 Gansevoort Street
    (Meatpacking)
untitledatthewhitney

Von
3 Bleecker Street
    (NoHo)
vonbar.com

Paris

....

Bistrot Paul Bert
18, Rue Paul Bert (11e)
01 43 72 24 01

Chez l'Ami Jean
27, Rue Malar (7e)
lamijean.fr/en

Boulangerie Julien
75, Rue Saint Honoré (1er)
1, Rue de Provence (9e)
boulangeriejulien.com

Du Pain et Des Idées
34, Rue Yves Toudic (10e)
dupainetdesidees.com/en

The Hemingway Bar at The Ritz
15, Place Vendome (1er)

About the Author

Photo by Lindsey Tramuta.

Amy Thomas is a Brooklyn-based writer, creative director, mother, and wife.